Speak with Confidence

Speak with Confidence

**Powerful Presentations
That Inform,
Inspire, and Persuade**

Dianna Booher

McGraw-Hill

New York   Chicago   San Francisco   Lisbon   London
Madrid   Mexico City   Milan   New Delhi
San Juan   Seoul   Singapore
Sydney   Toronto

The **McGraw·Hill** Companies

1 2 3 4 5 6 7 8 9 0 AGM/AGM 098765432

ISBN   978-0-07-140805-9
MHID 0-07-140805-3

This publication is designed to provide accurate and authoritative information in regard to the subject matter covered. It is sold with the understanding that the publisher is not engaged in rendering legal, accounting, or other professional service. If legal advice or other expert assistance is required, the services of a competent professional person should be sought.

—From a declaration of principles jointly adopted by a committee of the American Bar Association and a committee of publishers.

McGraw-Hill books are available at special quantity discounts to use as premiums and sales promotions, or for use in corporate training programs. For more information, please write to the Director of Special Sales, Professional Publishing, McGraw-Hill, Two Penn Plaza, New York, NY 10121-2298. Or contact your local bookstore.

Contents

Acknowledgments

This book is dedicated to the thousands of participants in client organizations who have put these presentation principles into practice. They have shown great willingness to be coached on the basics as well as the finer points that can take them to the next level in their careers.

Most important, these participants have been willing to try new ideas and then to share their experiences of success or failure in communicating with groups of 2 to 2000. They always keep me on target by asking for practical, usable tips and continually provide me with anecdotes on audience reactions and results. Thanks to each of you.

Thanks also to Polly Fuhrman, Jeffrey Booher, Sally Luttrell, Chris Casady, Karen Drake, and Vernon Rae for their research, observations, and work in coaching executives and professionals in the area of presentation skills—foundational research that eventually became part of this book.

Dianna Booher

Speak with Confidence

1
Wobbling in a Wired World

There is nothing wrong with having nothing to say—unless you insist on saying it.
UNKNOWN

In times like the present, men should utter nothing for which they would not willingly be responsible through time and in eternity.
ABRAHAM LINCOLN

Some speeches are like broiled lobster. You have to pick through an awful lot of bones to find any meat.
UNKNOWN

There is one thing stronger than all the armies in the world: an idea whose hour has come.
VICTOR HUGO

The tongue is more to be feared than the sword.
JAPANESE PROVERB

Communication pays off everywhere you turn. Speaking well is a measurable skill and valuable asset that can help you

- Gain respect, visibility, and recognition
- Influence and motivate others, strengthening your leadership position
- Cement relationships
- Build your reputation as an intelligent, interesting person

1

- Clarify your ideas and information to others
- Promote your company and its products or services
- Advance your career and earn financial rewards

Your potential to succeed in any relationship depends on your ability to communicate—whether it is conference-room talk, cafeteria talk, or pillow talk.

No longer is effective speaking a "plus" in the business world—it is now *expected*. And the higher one goes in a company, the more crucial this skill becomes. Today, public speaking is the norm for senior executives.

However, even if you are not a senior executive explaining a crisis to a group of line managers or investors, you often will find yourself speaking before peers in your day-to-day responsibilities as managers, engineers, lawyers, or marketers. And many of you speak for a living; that is, you talk to customers and clients daily to sell products or services. Your speaking success relates directly to your commission check.

We all know that it is not necessarily the brightest or most capable thinkers who get ahead. Often it is those who make a strong impact on people who end up in positions to promote them or buy from them. People who speak well generally are considered more intelligent, forceful, and respectable than their quieter counterparts.

Outside the business world, you will continue to find chances to put your speaking skills to use—at club fund-raisers, on political issues, at farewell gatherings for departing colleagues and friends, and on behalf of nonprofit organizations and causes.

Speaking well is no longer just a nice-to-have skill—it is a *must* for the successful individual.

COMMUNICATION, NOT JUST INFORMATION

Passing on information is not the problem. The problem is turning information into communication. Sitting through boring meeting after boring meeting while somebody stands to the left of a computer screen and narrates a slideshow in a darkened room just does not make the grade anymore—if it ever did. Connecting with an audience to push them to action or to a decision takes a very different mindset and skill than doling out data.

CLUELESS AND GOING IN CIRCLES

Another common problem is the presenter with presence and pizzazz on the platform—but who seems to be going nowhere in getting a point across. This is much ado about nothing. Everyone within earshot is entertained and motivated, but they walk away scratching their head, wondering, "What was the point? Am I supposed to do something differently? If so, how?"

PLATITUDES WITHOUT A PLATFORM

Some speakers have all the right answers, but no platform—that is, no credibility as a foundation to be heard and believed. Either the track record, the personality, the expertise, the action, the conviction, or the comportment of the speaker overshadows the message. As a result, the audience dismisses what he or she says without giving it full consideration.

PLATFORMS WITHOUT PLATITUDES

Then there's the opposite situation: People who find themselves in the limelight because of some event, crisis, or position they hold, and suddenly they have an audience—but no message. For example, they become a sports hero and then someone asks them for their views on parenting. They do not have a clue about what advice to give or even what has worked in their own relationships with parents or children. Or individuals become chief executive officers (CEOs), and the employee group asks them to outline their political views on immigration in the United States. Or movie stars hit the big time and reporters ask for their views on the relationship between pornography and crime. All these people have platforms—but not necessarily anything worthwhile to say.

RIGHT AUDIENCE, WRONG TALK

Sometimes professionals speaking before specific groups in the course of their jobs fail to take a situation and shape it into a clear message with a *specific* purpose for a *specific* audience. They take the same slide deck of information and dole it out to whoever asks for an update—any day for any reason.

RIGHT MESSAGE, WRONG MEDIUM

On other occasions, speakers may know what they want to convey and feel passionate about their subject, yet they select the wrong medium. Something that should have been communicated informally in a 15-minute "fireside chat" with a colloquial analogy is presented formally in a half-hour presentation with 27 slides, followed by a formal question-and-answer period relayed to a panel of staff experts.

EXPECTATIONS IN THE E-ERA

With a click of the mouse, users can access an Internet site and see the flashing glitz of full-color visuals, experience interactivity by having their personality profiled or their mortgage recalculated, or hear their favorite Mozart symphony or rock band. TV viewers can press the remote and watch live action as it unfolds in Afghanistan, Australia, or Angola. Employees at IBM Singapore can sit back and hear their manager via videoconference while he or she is vacationing in Puerto Rico.

Today's technology and everyday work and travel experiences have created an environment where audiences have seen and heard it all—before speakers ever open their mouths. Expectations are enormous for content, research, and visual support.

PLATFORM PLUSES AND MINUSES

All these issues are just that—issues. They can be platform pluses or minuses depending on whether you consider them or ignore them in preparing for your own speaking opportunities.

The pluses mean that you have the power of technology to research your topic, to produce the exact visual you need to clarify your point, to transport that visual to just about any location, and to deliver your message around the world instantly.

The minuses, however, are that the same technology can tempt you to fade into a slide narrator with a monochrome personality in an era that demands presence and dynamism.

HOW THIS BOOK CAN HELP

This book offers speaking tips for people in a variety of situations:

- Executives, managers, or other professionals presenting information to their colleagues, clients, or suppliers as a part of their daily jobs
- Technical experts wanting to "translate" highly complex data and information to nontechnical groups
- Salespeople making sales presentations to their clients
- Company representatives speaking to civic and industry groups to gain visibility and create goodwill
- Trainers
- Facilitators of meetings and videoconferences
- Emcees and panel moderators
- Professional speakers

You'll notice that the tips in this book are grouped into 16 chapters covering all the basic issues facing these groups of people: building rapport with an audience, creating platform presence with a dynamic delivery, creating and organizing the content, practicing the presentation, selling the ideas, telling a good story to illustrate key points, creating and using appropriate visual support, handling questions with authority, building in interactivity for retention and impact, handling the logistics of site preparation, dealing with problems such as equipment failure or memory blocks or distractions, and finally, evaluating effectiveness and asking for coaching.

Chapters 1 through 5, 7 through 13, and 16 contain tips that apply to almost every speaker. You may want to refer to the remaining chapters on presenting technical information, emceeing, and videoconferencing only when you have a specific need.

Considering the hectic pace of today's business presenter, I have selected a pick-up, put-down format. That is, you can go immediately to the chapter you need and just skim the bold tips for the key ideas. When you need more elaboration on an idea, help yourself to the explanation that follows.

SIX STEPS TO SUCCESS

The roadmap to success in speaking with confidence before a group involves these six key steps:

Step 1: Analyze your audience and determine your purpose.

Step 2: Research and collect your information.

Step 3: Organize your ideas and information.

Step 4: Add the "finishing touches" to the content and structure.

Step 5: Prepare any supporting visuals.

Step 6: Practice your delivery, including interactivity and questions and answers.

The reason for failure in many cases in that some speakers start with step 5 as the foundational step. Then, with a deadline looming large, they try to mold the audience and the rest of the content around the visuals. Practice happens only in their head with a mental walk-through before they "wing it" for real before a group that can make or break their career—or at least give input to crucial decisions or projects.

This is *not* an ideal situation or plan.

Yet, most people have the natural ingredients to be effective presenters. For example:

- Do you enjoy telling people what you think on a particular subject?
- Are you sensitive to others' reactions to what you say?
- Do you talk with your hands?
- Do you look people in the eye when you talk to them?
- Are you typically animated in conversation, moving with energy that seems to flow unconsciously from you?
- Do you like telling people what you have learned so that they can benefit, too?
- Do you think visually?

- Can you explain a complicated idea or a complex piece of equipment in fairly simple terms?

- Do you wish that you could help others understand things as clearly as you do?

- Can you keep your cool under pressure?

- Do you tend to "get up on a soapbox" when talking about a topic or cause that is important to you?

- Is there a little bit of cheerleader in you?

- Do you feel proud to learn that things turned out well for someone who took your advice in handling a situation?

- After meetings, do you tend to want a summary of what has been said? Do you create one yourself?

- Have you ever thought that you would like to be an actor or a singer?

If you answered "yes" to even half of these questions, chances are that you will make a great speaker. Either you already possess much of the natural skill required, or you exhibit the motivation needed for learning to communicate effectively one-on-one or in front of groups.

The rest of this book will provide the practical tips to do just that.

2

Rapport with Your Audience— The "Like" Link

*Don't confuse being stimulating with being
blunt.* BARBARA WALTERS

Speech is a picture of the mind. JOHN RAY

*Talk to a man about himself and he will listen
for hours.* BENJAMIN DISRAELI

*A voice is a human gift; it should be cherished
and used, to utter fully human speech as possible. Powerlessness and silence go together.*
MARGARET ATWOOD

*It is better to speak from a full heart and an
empty head than from a full head and an empty
heart.* FROM THE *DUBLIN OPINION*

Connections create credibility. To put it simply, people are much more apt
to believe you if they like you.

Haven't you observed speakers who had great messages but who lost
your respect because of their arrogance? On the other hand, how about
those poor ramblers who had tremendous difficulty organizing their
thoughts and feelings but whose words moved you because you liked them
personally?

7

Think how much of any President's success can be attributed to personal popularity. Consider your favorite local news anchors or sports broadcasters. How much of their success can be attributed to viewer opinions such as, "He seems like a nice guy" or "She comes across as warm and intelligent"?

My office recently made a choice of "personality" over "academic credentials" in hiring a new instructor. After serious consideration of a candidate with a Ph.D. in journalism and 8 years' experience teaching technical writing to adults, my colleagues and I settled on our second applicant, who has a master's degree and a likable personality. While we would have been proud to present the Ph.D. to our clients, we unfortunately detected a cynical, arrogant attitude during our interviews with her that we feared would be abrasive to her audiences—our clients. We based our final decision on the truism that people do not like to listen to people they do not like.

Personality traits and the attitudes of speakers either attract or repel audiences.

TIP 1: Establish Integrity Through Third-Party Endorsements

Try to relate to audience

Audiences want to listen to a speaker who holds similar ethical values and reflects attitudes about life similar to theirs. They want to be able to believe the speaker when he or she states facts, shares data, and relates experiences. Yet, unless the audience has had an opportunity to know the presenter personally, integrity remains largely an unknown trait and leaves a great gulf of skepticism that only evidence or time will overcome.

One way to decrease the distance is to transfer trust by association. That is, establish a connection with another person or group that the audience *does* trust, and convey that connection early. You can make the connection either by providing written material about the speaker or by having another person whose judgment the group trusts give a personal introduction.

TIP 2: Be Genuine

Audiences want to know that what they see is what they will get. A few months ago I heard a speaker at a convention make several offers to address participants' questions and concerns after the session. He seemed genuinely interested in making himself available to anyone in the audience. However, when someone approached him with a question a few hours later, his brusque manner let the audience member know that he did not have time to "waste." The speaker's hypocrisy and lack of warmth glared like a neon sign.

Audiences sense concern and genuineness. They typically do not warm up to speakers who hide behind a "facts only" presentation—one that is formal, emotionless, or indifferent. In general, be willing to share who you are with your audience and to laugh at your weaknesses, your mistakes, and your humanity.

TIP 3: Show Enthusiasm for Your Topic

Intrest

Don't be afraid to show enthusiasm for your subject. "I'm excited about being here today" says good things to an audience. It generally means that you are confident, you have something of value to say, and you are prepared to state your case clearly. Boredom is contagious. Audiences get it from speakers who resist being "too emotional" about their ideas and the outcome of their presentation.

Even the most mundane topic can be interesting to an audience if you show a little creativity and curiosity. For example, consider the cabbage supply at the Loyola site. Is the price higher or lower than last year? Is the product more or less profitable than the competitor's? Do the grocery store owners agree or disagree about its quality and nutritional value? Do both the rich and poor alike buy it? Why or why not?

If you need more incentive to show enthusiasm, consider the collective value (salary per hour) of audience members' time. Is what you have to say

> Come on, let's see those hands. How many of you are surprised about the current price of cabbage in Kansas?

Boredom is contagious—audiences get it from speakers.

worth $X per minute? Somebody evidently thought so in asking you to make the presentation. This notion should infuse you with confidence and enthusiasm for your subject.

Do not equate enthusiasm with hysteria, however. Do not intimidate your audience by forcing them to raise their hands if they will contribute at least $X to your cause, bring a friend to next week's meeting, or stop letting their spouse beat them at poker. How much enthusiasm is too much? You have to be the judge. Again, let genuineness be your guide. If you are emotional because you really feel conviction about what you are saying, then you are on solid ground. When you feel that you are faking it, it is time to back off and cool down.

TIP 4: Sprinkle Humility Among the Expertise

This characteristic confuses many beginning speakers. On the one hand, audiences want the speaker to be knowledgeable about the subject. On the other hand, they do not want a speaker to be arrogant about his or her expertise. You have to determine for yourself the proper balance between expertise (which establishes credibility) and humility (which makes you likable rather than arrogant).

On occasion, you *will* have to sell the audience on your competence to speak on a given subject. When you do, select experiences, ideas, and illustrations that convey your range of expertise without sounding either egotistical or falsely modest.

Keep in mind that there are ways to show humility other than an overly modest presentation of credentials. You can acknowledge your audience's expertise with a statement such as, "Frankly, I'm a little puzzled about speaking in front of a group such as yours. Many of you have as much or more experience with [the topic] than I do. I'm hoping to share a different perspective on [the topic] for your consideration." And be sure to credit your information sources and any ideas borrowed from others.

In short, a speaker's success rests on three things: likableness, conviction, and competence.

TIP 5: Demonstrate Goodwill and a Desire to Give Value

One of the most damning responses an audience can give when asked what a speaker had to say is, "Nothing much." Consider every presentation you make as a commitment to give something of value. If you do not have time to prepare or do not feel compelled to make the effort, then turn down the invitation to speak.

The audience has to believe that you have their best interests at heart, have not arrived on the scene with the intention of boring them, and are giving them information designed to help, not hinder, them. Even those speaking as a "prelude" to selling their services (such as those selected to speak at an industry conference or national convention) must give their audiences valuable information rather than only unclear "teasers" to tempt them to buy. When they give solid information rather than only fluff, they actually report better results in follow-up discussions.

To do otherwise in a technical situation among your own colleagues can mean disaster. People typically are not impressed with the fact that you know what you are supposed to know. They are impressed that you are willing *to help them know* what you know.

TIP 6: Develop and Display a Sense of Humor

You do not have to be a stand-up comic or even aim to entertain your audience to inject some humor into your presentation. Just adopt a light approach, an attitude of spontaneity, and a willingness to see humor in the ordinary things that happen.

For instance, instead of getting upset when the projector light goes out during your slide show, reward your audience with an unscheduled break while you bring things under control. Rather than getting stressed out because the previous speaker stole your thunder, comment on his or her good taste in reciting your favorite anecdote. Instead of getting frazzled after dropping your note cards, quip, "I thought I'd shuffle them halfway through to see if the ideas flow better that way." The use of cartoons or humorous quotations also reveals your sense of humor.

However you spark the humor inside, your audience needs to see and hear it.

TIP 7: Don't Sermonize

Few people have all the answers. Even when you have all the information as a presenter, audience members typically like to separate the substantiated facts from the sermonizing.

Granted, for some presentations, your role *is* to persuade and interpret. However, do not confuse persuasion with sermons. Sermonizing stems from both word choice and tone: "You really ought to . . ." "I was afraid you'd be disappointed when the decision was made to . . ." "Ignoring these data early on was a serious error in judgment—one that any engineer worth his or her paycheck should have been able to identify." Some comments do not endear you to a group—even if they are not the target of your tirade.

TIP 8: Meet People Individually Before You Begin Your Presentation

Introducing yourself to various people in the group and asking about their expectations for the meeting or session or their interest in the topic or role in the project you may be addressing builds rapport for several reasons: It says that you are aware of their individual presence and do not just view them as a group—that you care about their individual concerns or interests. Chitchat gives you a chance to find a common bond—a mutual acquaintance, viewpoint, interest, history, or goal. Finally, they come to see you as a "regular" person—someone like themselves, someone they can believe.

TIP 9: Refer to People by Name During Your Presentation

Arrive early to meet and greet audience members, engaging them in a little chitchat about what they are hoping to learn or hear during your talk, what their role in the organization is, what key projects they are working on, or what mutual friends or colleagues you may have. Not only does this build rapport with individuals, but you also will learn valuable information that will help you further customize your remarks.

A specific reference by name—particularly, if you can add some further comment about what the person said, did, or believes—is like a personal pat on the back in front of a group. And when any single person in the group receives praise, the entire group generally feels the stroke. However, the reference does not necessarily need to be praise. "Geri, didn't you tell me you'd worked at Universal yourself a few years ago? So, of course, you know also that the culture there is . . ." is an audience-involving technique that says to the group "That speaker obviously isn't on automatic pilot. He or she is aware of us as individuals who'll need to live with this merger."

TIP 10: Forget the Old Adage "Never Thank an Audience"

Years ago, the conventional wisdom was that speakers should never thank an audience at the conclusion of a presentation. In fact, drama and speech professors insisted, "The audience should thank you, the speaker." Of course, thanking an audience is appropriate. You may want to thank them for their invitation, for the platform or forum, for listening, for their hospitality, for their participation in any interactivity, or for considering their response to any action you are proposing. A genuine, heart-felt "thank you" always builds rapport with a group.

3

Platform Presence—
Your Dynamic Delivery

*Poise: The ability to be at ease conspicuously or
the ability to be ill at ease naturally.*
UNKNOWN

*Head table: Here is where speakers take their
seat, pleased to be looked at, too scared to eat.*
RICHARD ARMOUR

*Three things matter in a speech: who says it,
how he says it, and what he says . . . and of the
three, the last matters the least.*   LORD MORLEY

On occasion, your speaking "platform" may be an elevator—when your
boss steps on at the 60th floor, turns to you, and says, "So how's the big project going?" and you have 120 seconds to give a status report before he or
she steps off into the lobby.

On other occasions, you may be standing before a group of 2000 customers at an industry meeting or presenting your annual goals and budget
in a small conference before 7 colleagues. Your "platform" in all these situations is both portable and powerful. Any of these speaking opportunities
has the potential to create career momentum or mishap for you.

Presence may be difficult to define, but it is easy to spot. Most people
know it when they see it. It is a manner of moving and interacting that commands attention and creates confidence in the speaker and increases credibility for the content.

NERVOUSNESS

TIP 11: Accept Nervousness as Part of the Process

Stage fright often begins long before a performer takes the stage. For most of us, the condition sets in the moment we accept an invitation to make a presentation. And generally, the longer we have to anticipate the event, the more prolonged and severe the symptoms.

The typical person is uncomfortable in a public speaking forum. Neither rank nor personality is a differentiator. In years of coaching on presentation skills, I have had some of the most outstanding executives tell me that they still feel uncomfortable in front of a group—even after hundreds of presentations before employee, stockholder, or industry groups. And even life-of-the-party-type salespeople who give a great presentation sometimes walk away with sweaty palms and knots in their stomachs.

At times our fears are rational; sometimes not. We may fear that our subject or information is not quite what the audience expects, needs, or wants. Or we fear that they will attack the quality of our performance or challenge our credentials, asking a question we cannot answer. Or we visualize ourselves making a misstatement or omitting key information. Even if we know our subject well and feel confident about our qualifications to speak, we may fear that we will perform so badly that we will embarrass ourselves. Surely the group will notice our nervousness and our embarrassment.

If we have no other cause for fear, some of us worry that we won't have adequate preparation time or that some circumstance beyond our control (such as the audiovisual equipment going berserk) will foul things up.

If any of these are fears of yours, you are in good company. Even the most famous movie stars, singers, and politicians admit to fear before certain performances. And political and business speakers particularly experience a specific form of anxiety that accompanies presenting a script prepared by someone else to an audience ready to challenge their ideas.

When you hear someone claim not to be nervous before giving a presentation, you are probably in for a boring talk. Presenters who lack a certain amount of anxiety do not have enough adrenalin flow to push them to peak performance. They are too confident and relaxed to do their best job.

TIP 12: Use Fear to Push You to a Peak Performance

The secret to a great presentation is performing despite the nervousness—in fact, making your jitters work *for* you. Imagine the tension and extra adrenalin pumping through you as catalysts to a great performance.

Yes, on occasion you may feel that you have lost control of your body. You may experience one or more of the following symptoms: rapid pulse, sweaty palms, dry mouth, buckling knees, twitching muscles, shortness of breath, quivering voice, and queasiness. No matter how nervous you are, however, never tell your audience. If they sense your discomfort, they will worry about you—much like a parent does when a daughter mounts the school stage as Cinderella. Your admission may direct them to your shaking hands when they should be listening to your words. Remember, however, typically your nervousness does not show.

What sometimes throws off a typically confident nature when we speak before a group is lack of feedback. In one-on-one conversation, we receive immediate feedback—the listener's raised eyebrow, frown, argument, smile, nod, or confirmation of our ideas. When speaking before a group, we often feel lost without this feedback. It is like crossing a shallow river when you can't see the stepping-stones beneath the surface; you're a little nervous with each step until your foot touches the solid surface.

In attempting to control nervousness, remind yourself not ever to give in. I compare it to a situation I occasionally find myself in when traveling across the country. I arrive in a strange city at night, rent a car, and drive to some remote motel in the suburbs for the next day's meeting or consulting assignment. While walking from my car to my room, I struggle to remain calm. As I move away from the lights of the parking lot, my stride gets a little faster. The sight of a shadow or form along my path makes my footsteps quicken as fear threatens to overtake me. The scenario ends with a speedy lunge for the night lock.

Maybe you have found yourself in a similar situation, where you knew that if fear overtook you, you would be in trouble. You take a deep breath and refuse to let your nerves get the best of you. Show the same resolve when giving a presentation—refuse to take that first step toward letting yourself fall apart. Instead of thinking about how you might embarrass yourself, concentrate on your subject. Recall and rehearse your key points rather than your key obstacles.

TIP 13: Use Positive Self-Talk Rather than Focusing on the Fear

One way to build your confidence is to remember that you have been asked to give the presentation; someone believes in your capability and subject-matter expertise. Remind yourself that if others in the audience were more knowledgeable than you, they would have been asked to make the presentation.

Fear is a learned response. A two-year-old does not fear walking into the street until someone yanks him or her back, warning him or her of the danger. We learn the same fear of public speaking the first time a classmate stands up to recite a poem, has a memory lapse, and gets flustered, causing snickers to erupt throughout the room. And because fear is learned, it can be unlearned—or at least controlled.

TIP 14: Find Your Fans

It is part of human nature to be cowed by negative personality types. This goes for presenters also. They look into the audience and see the one glum face staring at them, looking either bored, angry, or impatient. The tendency is to play to that one cynic, trying to persuade, soften, lead, motivate, empower, enlighten, or appease—whatever it takes to turn the gloom to bloom.

However, it rarely happens. And in the process, you grow more nervous and rattled and sometimes lose the rest of the audience.

It is far better to find your fans up front. If you know you have supportive people in the group, focus on those faces. These positive high achievers sport a different expression. They smile. They blink. They nod. They move. They shift. They are the let's-keep-an-open-mind, let's-make-this-work kind of people. They do not just suck the energy out of you—they give some back. These people have a contagious spirit that generates enthusiasm for at least a discussion, if not acceptance, of your ideas.

TIP 15: Play Mental Games of "What's the Worst?" to Overcome Disabling Fear

Another trick for calming yourself is to consider the unnerving experience in light of eternity. What is the worst that can happen? What will it all matter a year from now? In fact, if you goof, who will even remember it tomorrow? In the big scheme of things, your presentation will prove minuscule.

In fact, my husband often translates irrational fears into a good laugh with observations such as this one: "I can see it now in *USA TODAY*— 'Dianna Booher used an anecdote for which one-third of the audience didn't understand the point. She also arrived wearing a navy-blue suit on which the flight attendant spilled a soda just as she was leaving the plane and. . . .' " You get the picture. Plan, then learn to put things in perspective.

TIP 16: Use Physical Exercise and Activity to Release Nervous Tension

Following are some things you can do to alleviate both the physical and mental symptoms of nervousness:

- Take a few deep breaths and exhale slowly. (This forces the muscles to relax a bit, increases the flow of oxygen to the brain, and lowers the pulse rate.)
- Let all the muscles in your body go limp, then tense them, and then let them go limp again.
- Clench your fists and then relax them.
- Let your arms dangle limply, rotate your wrists, and then shake your hands, like in the Hokey Pokey.
- Drop your jaw and move it from side to side. Yawn.
- Drop your jaw, as though yawning, and keep your tongue flat against the bottom of your mouth. Suck in a few short breaths, and you will yawn yourself into relaxation.
- Roll your head, shoulders, or both.
- Go limp like Raggedy Ann and then straighten up. Repeat.
- Select an object and stare at it for a long while, concentrating on relaxing.
- Take a brisk walk or jog before arriving at the event.

Select whichever mental or physical tricks are likely to work best for you in a particular situation. The idea is to transport yourself from terror to fear to tension to mere stimulation. It is in the stimulation mode that you will be best able to inspire or motivate your audience.

TIP 17: Concentrate on Your Audience Rather Than on Yourself to Reduce Tension

How will your ideas help your audience to improve their lives or at least increase their knowledge? Learn to appreciate the energy this tension creates; think of the swarm of butterflies in your stomach as a wellspring of creativity pushing upward to make your presentation one to remember. Feel passionate about your subject. Prepare well. Psych yourself up for the positive results your presentation is sure to bring.

TIP 18: Don't Let Fear Mean Mediocrity

Do not settle for being an "average" presenter, one who is scared into conformity. Do not risk losing your audience with a boringly straitlaced performance—one that is not too passionate, not too loud, not too flashy, not too funny, not too controversial, not too emotional, not too formal, not too informal—not too *anything*. Never look around your organization to "what everybody else does" when they present and conform to mediocrity.

See what everyone else does, and do *not* do it. Your success depends more often on being different—on excelling.

TIP 19: Be Better Than "Natural"

Larry Rogers, a lawyer friend of mine, specializes in corporate finance. He is always dressed impeccably in a pinstriped suit and white shirt, but he is extremely shy. When joining our social circle at a restaurant, he nods and smiles on entering the room, takes a seat, and never says another word unless spoken to.

Four years into my acquaintanceship with Larry, I was invited (by someone else) to conduct a seminar at his company. The subject of public speaking and eloquence came up during a break at the seminar. Several of the participants commented that they wished they could be eloquent on their feet. One member of the group turned to me and raved, "Speaking of eloquence, you should hear one of our legal VPs. He's fabulous. When he makes a presentation, he has the audience eating out of his hand. He can think on his feet, his language and diction are flawless, and his wit is charming. He's awesome!" Several others chimed in their agreement.

"Oh, really?" I responded. "Would I have met this person in an earlier session?"

"I don't know. But if you haven't, you definitely should meet him. He's absolutely the best speaker in our company. Everybody knows him because of that. He's always the corporate spokesperson for everything."

"What's his name?" I probed.

"Larry Rogers."

Anyone—no matter how shy—can blossom as a speaker without abandoning his or her natural personality but rather by building on its strengths.

When coaches suggest that speakers show more energy and animation in their body language or voice, they often respond, "But that's just not me. That's just not natural." Often presenters confuse "sincere" and "relaxed" with boring and low energy. That is, they have a mental picture of themselves as "naturally" shy and unanimated. However, in my 22 years of coaching experience, I find just the opposite more often in such situations. These same people are *naturally* animated and energetic when talking with their friends at lunch or with their families on the phone. Rather, they become their *unnatural* selves in front of a group.

Be yourself, yes, but be your *best* self—animated, energetic, and passionate about your topic and your purpose to move the group to action or decision.

I once coached an instructor who was seeking to improve the energy in her voice and body during presentations. During the session, she kept saying that she couldn't be more animated—"It just isn't me." Yet, when we finished the session and chatted informally for a few minutes, she unconsciously lapsed into her natural speaking style. While describing her recent dinner with an old friend, she seemed transformed—her voice grew livelier, her face glowed, her eyes sparkled, and she gestured expressively to illustrate her points. "Freeze!" I shouted. "Look in the mirror; listen to your voice!"

After several similar interruptions that evening, she came to realize that she was naturally animated, enthusiastic person. Her stiff before-a-group performance was really her *un*natural self.

The idea is to catch yourself being natural while talking on the phone to a neighbor about the barking dog next door, to your family about your trip to the auto mechanic, to a friend about the embarrassment of forgetting

Be your natural self—not your unnatural self—in front of a group.

someone's name, to a colleague about a movie scene you thought was hilarious. Learn to catch yourself in these situations. Then think about what it feels like, and listen to how your voice sounds. Then try to model that feeling and tone when speaking to a group.

This is not to say that we are animated and enthusiastic every time we utter a word. You don't say, "The garbage needs to be taken out this morning" with the same fervor as "I just won a trip to Europe!"

Learn to distinguish the *natural* you—the animated, energetic person you are with friends in a relaxed situation—from the *un*natural you, the person you become when feeling self-conscious in front of a group. Then be the natural you when speaking to a group and remind yourself that you are simply talking to an audience of more than one.

TIP 20: Make Your Presentation Both a Performance and a Conversation

Performance focuses on the subject matter, regardless of the audience's needs. *Conversation* focuses on what the listener needs and wants to hear. A successful presentation requires both perspectives. Your style should not be a rambling discourse, which makes for a bad conversation of any type, but a fresh, straightforward style of speaking one on one.

All of us, every day, act. According to Shakespeare, "All the world's a stage, and all the men and women merely players." We usually adapt our delivery when we are around others, becoming a little more formal than when singing in the shower. Good speakers, however, try to be themselves—with an edge. If you do not normally pop off witty lines, do not try it in front of an audience. If you do not use slang and colloquialisms in everyday speech, do not do so in a presentation. Audiences are sensitive to this kind of phoniness; they can tell it isn't you.

Of course, personal conversations and public speaking are *not* exactly the same. You feel more vulnerable in front of a group because several people, rather than just a single individual, have given you their attention. Because people have taken time away from their normal schedules, you feel pressure to make what you say count—to be structured and logical. Finally, you may feel in limbo because the usual pattern of feedback is altered. In natural conversation, you get an immediate reaction and receive immediate feedback: "Oh, really? Then what? You're kidding! Why is that?" Such cues guide your delivery and inspire you to continue. In public speaking, you cannot depend on such verbal prompts to tell you how you are doing and if you are coming across as you intend.

The trick of effective speaking, then, is to combine the best of both worlds—speaking and performing. Talk—only to a larger audience. Learn to feel your natural style, its level of animation and enthusiasm.

TIP 21: Assume a Friendly Audience

If you assume the members of your audience are waiting to catch you in an error or argue with you, you'll likely feel nervous and may even sound hostile during your presentation.

Based on my own experience and that of many other professional speakers, I assure you that audiences want speakers to do well. After all, they have taken time out of their busy schedules, and they are hoping to gain something from your presentation. Even those who are forced to attend will be pleasantly surprised if you give them something of value or entertain them.

To reassure yourself that your audience members are friendly and positive, arrive early and talk with people individually. Chat about the occasion, their trip to the site, what their work entails, common acquaintances—anything that lets them see you as a nice person who is interested in them. Such small talk also allows you to see them as familiar "friends" who will welcome and benefit from what you have to say.

If you do not have an opportunity to talk casually with individual audience members before taking the stage, do so with the whole group just before beginning your presentation. Ask if they are comfortable. Is the room too warm? Too dark? Solicit applause for someone who had a great deal to do with planning the meeting. Compliment those in attendance on their dedication to the issue at hand: "You must be the kind of people who care how our community's youth spend their leisure time."

Even your body language conveys how you feel about your audience. If you feel that they are friendly, you will walk over and stand closer to them.

Assume a friendly audience.

If you are uncomfortable with them, you will hide behind the lectern or table and lean away.

Finally, do not be discouraged by frowns or silences. Silence means deep thought and agreement as often as it does boredom. Here is proof: An engineer in one of my audiences worried me even before I began my talk. When she entered the room, she spoke to no one and made negligible eye contact with me or anyone else the whole morning. She propped her chin in her hand and doodled on a scratch pad throughout the presentation. I tried every technique I could come up with to involve her, to draw a smile, to elicit a sign of interest or understanding. Finally, assuming her to be a lost cause, I gave up. Imagine my surprise when I later read her evaluation of the session: "Absolutely the best presentation I've ever attended. Should be required for every engineer in the company." So much for reading body language! All faces do not reflect thoughts.

Yes, it is important to be sensitive to your audience members' body language. At the least, assume they will listen respectfully; at best, they will agree with what you have to say. With this perspective, your delivery will sound relaxed and upbeat.

POSTURE AND GESTURES THAT HIGHLIGHT

TIP 22: Make Your Body Language Consistent with Your Words

When an audience senses inconsistency in a speaker's message, what do they rely on for the truth? Picture this scene on the evening news: A reporter extends the microphone toward the mayor of the city and asks for his response to charges of fraud in city government. The mayor denounces the charges as "ridiculous" yet fidgets as he talks and keeps his eyes downcast. Which would you believe—the mayor's verbal denial or his body language? Why?

When the message seems inconsistent with nonverbal cues (eye contact, posture, facial expression, or movement), body language and tone typically trump our words. You either look enthusiastic about your subject or you do not. The impact of the visual element on your audience is difficult to shake.

TIP 23: Use Your Eyes to Build Intimacy with Audience Members One by One Randomly Around the Room

Eye contact, or the lack thereof, is a speaker's most noticeable mannerism. Eye contact establishes a bond. You have signaled your interest in that person and conveyed your sincerity about what you are saying.

Guillaume de Sallusie, a sixteenth-century poet, called the eyes "the windows of the soul," and there is plenty of proof of the power of eye contact in communications. Consider these everyday comments on the significance our culture attaches to eye contact: "I bet he couldn't look you in the eye and say that" or "She gave me the evil eye as I walked through the door." Lovers spend hours staring into each other's eyes, sharing feelings words cannot express. Enemies watch their opponents' eyes to determine their next move. Tackles watch the quarterback's eyes to predict a fake. Members of a negotiating team sit around a table discussing the proposed terms and interpreting each other's reactions, as reflected in their eyes.

Effective eye contact is crucial to a speaker's success. Here are some dos and don'ts you will want to heed. First, the don'ts:

- Don't stare at only one or two people or at a spot in the back of the room.
- Don't let your eyes flit around the room as if you are afraid to look at anyone's face.
- Don't stare at your notes, your laptop screen, the table, your visuals, your shoes, or the floor.
- Don't read from a script so that you can manage only momentary glances at the audience between thoughts.
- Don't look around, between, or over listeners' heads.
- Don't stand so far away from your audience that they cannot see your eyes even when you're looking at them.

Now the dos:

- Do deliver your points to individuals around the room. Focus on individual audience members to establish personal contact. Let your eyes fall on an individual, hold that contact, make your point, and then move to the next pair of eyes. You establish eye contact while delivering a point, a phrase, a punch line, or an illustration to that person, and then you move your eyes to the next person for the next point. Delivering one or two sentences to each person establishes a bond of intimacy with individual listeners.
- Do glance randomly around the room from time to time, taking in the whole audience in one sweep.
- Do face one section of the room while completing a point. Then move to the next section of the audience to linger and select individuals for closer contact.

TIP 24: Think of Eye Contact as a Form of Paragraphing

When you break eye contact with an individual or even the entire audience at once and change your pose and glance—maybe to look pensively or to glance from side to side for effect or to look at the floor and shrug your shoulders or to examine a prop or to study disappointing numbers on a slide—then return your glance to a different person, you signal a new thought. The effect is much the same as what happens when a reader comes to white space and a new paragraph or heading on a document. The reader stops mentally and refocuses on the new idea or angle.

When speaking, you do not have printed cues such as paragraphs. Your body language must serve the same purpose.

TIP 25: Don't Eagle-Eye the Decision Maker

Particularly when trying to sell an idea to an internal audience or an external client, do not focus solely on the decision maker. The message you convey to the rest of the group is that they are unimportant and their input unnecessary. Their hostility typically unfolds during the question-and-answer period.

TIP 26: Use a Confident, Balanced Posture to Convey Authority

Stand with your weight equally balanced on both feet (but without your knees locked) and with shoulders and arms comfortably at your side or extended, not rigid.

Some women have been taught a "modeling" walk and pose, whereby the heel of one foot is brought into the side of the other foot. They often look as if they are pulling away from their audience. Not a very impressive, authoritative stance.

Some men adopt the aggressive gunslinger pose, whereby both arms extend slightly to the side, as if they are about to draw a pistol from a hip holster and take a shot from behind the OK Corral at sundown. Not a very relaxed or welcoming stance.

The most confident, authoritative posture is somewhere in between these two extremes. Pay attention to your feet—what you do with your feet dictates your lower body posture.

TIP 27: Use an Open Posture to Invite Participation

On occasion, you may want to reduce your "authority." That is, during a question-and-answer period or in a meeting with a client when inviting feedback on your proposal, you may want to appear more informal to encourage a dialogue.

With an unbuttoned jacket, hands in the pocket, and perhaps even leaning or sitting on the side of a conference table as you talk, you can strike a more casual posture that invites discussion and questions.

TIP 28: Be Aware That Gestures and Mannerisms Either Support or Sabotage What You Say

Gestures and mannerisms can either convince your audience of your sincerity or antagonize them. Imagine yourself in an airport, with conversations going on all around you, and you yourself engaged in a farewell to a friend. All of a sudden, the man and woman sitting next to you begin to wave their arms dramatically, their fingers urgently punching the air. Immediately, your attention is diverted from your own conversation to this couple. Why do their words not distract you, but their gestures do? That's the power of gestures and mannerisms; often, movement speaks louder than words.

You may be completely serious, passionate, and confident about what you have to say, but your audience may perceive you as insincere because of poor eye contact, slouched posture, a bored expression, or weak gestures.

TIP 29: Study the Meanings of Common Gestures, Mannerisms, and Postures to Increase Your Awareness of Your Own Body Language

The following list of common gestures, mannerisms, and postures is organized by what attitude they convey to the audience:

A Dictatorial Approach

- Crossed arms
- Pounding fist
- Hands on hips
- Pointing index finger
- Hands behind back
- Karate chops in the air
- Hands in a "steeple" position

Openness

- Open hands, palms up
- Large arm gestures

- Removing your glasses
- Moving from behind the lectern or table
- Stepping off the platform
- Walking toward and into the audience
- Leaning forward on your toes or in your chair
- Hand-to-face gestures
- Unbuttoned suit coat or shirt collar, loosened tie
- Head tilted to the side

Insecurity/Nervousness

- Gripping the lectern or audiovisual equipment
- Chewing on objects, such as pencil erasers
- Biting fingernails
- Biting lips
- Continual throat clearing
- Hands in pockets
- Hands covering mouth
- Clenched fists
- Lack of eye contact
- Jingling keys or coins in pocket
- Removing glasses and then replacing them
- Strumming fingers
- Touching ears
- Playing with hair, mustache, or beard
- Twisting rings or other jewelry
- Rocking back and forth or from side to side
- Tossing chalk, marker, or pointer in air
- Rubbing hand across forehead and through hair
- Rubbing back of neck
- Picking at imaginary or real lint on clothes, flesh

Emphasis

- Underscoring a point on a visual aid
- Large arm movements from the shoulder

- Dramatic pauses
- Lifted eyebrows
- Head poised in reflective tilt
- Bouncing gently on toes
- Animated facial expression

Arrogance

- Hands on lapels or hem of suit jacket
- Steepled fingers
- Preening gestures (patting hair, adjusting clothing)
- Pointing finger in lecturing fashion

Whatever your gestures, they serve three main purposes: to release nervous tension, to gain and hold the audience's attention, and to underscore your message.

Appropriateness of gestures is also of paramount importance. When delivering an inspirational message to motivate an audience to action, the use of full-blown gestures, excited movements, and a strong voice would be natural and supportive. With a group of older government officials, however, you may want to replace the rah-rah motions with extended eye contact, clenched fists, and a determined glint in your eye. In a small room, large gestures may make you feel like an elephant in a furniture store. In a large room, small gestures will make you look like a bewildered child.

To sum up, negative gestures and mannerisms include both a slouched posture and a rigid stance with no movement; small, limp gestures; fidgeting with clothes or objects; and word fillers such as *aahhs* and *uhs*. Positive gestures include a comfortable posture; big, open hands and arms; animated facial expressions; and effective pauses rather than word fillers.

How do you break bad habits and form new ones? With conscious effort. For example, clasp your hands together, with your fingers interlocked. Is your left thumb or your right thumb on top? Now switch the positions of your thumbs—put the opposite thumb on top. Feels awkward, right? Any conscious change will seem awkward at first, but that does not mean it will look awkward to your audience.

TIP 30: Become Conscious of What Your Body Language Says When You're in Front of a Group

Your upper-body posture is controlled primarily by what you do with your arms. Your posture and your gestures are difficult to separate. They make a total statement.

I work with many people who are completely unaware of their body language until they see themselves on video for the first time. For example, some people stand with their head intensely protruding forward as if they are about to scold the audience. Others stand in a slouched position as though they are exhausted from marching through the desert for days without rest. Others hug, pat, and squeeze themselves when they speak. Still others either stand rigid as if locked in a straightjacket or sway back and forth as if they are a shy teenager about to ask their first date to the prom.

Look at yourself in the mirror and see how it feels to stand with your arms relaxed loosely at your side or with your elbows slightly bent. It may *feel* awkward, but it does not *look* awkward. Simply stand there, looking in the mirror, and get used to the various postures that both look and feel appropriate so that you do not *feel* awkward with that same natural posture, gesture, or stance in front of a group.

TIP 31: Try Increasing Your Volume to Release Your Natural Inclination to Gesture

People who speak softly also tend to use few gestures. The louder your volume, the more energy you require. The more energy you require, the more natural it will seem to use gestures to emphasize key points. Consider the last argument you had with a family member—arms waving, scrunched-up faces, wagging heads. It is difficult to use big, open gestures with a tiny voice. The reverse is also true. Raising your volume usually will improve your gesturing.

If you have taken to heart advice about being conversational, most of your gestures will be appropriate and effective. Your instinctive intellectual and emotional energy will reflect your feelings about your subject. Again, the key is to catch yourself being natural—your best self—in front of a group.

TIP 32: Stage Your Points So That Your Audience Can Follow You

Actors call the planned use of physical space and movement *staging*. Even those well-planned community events you attend where the mayor presents awards to the local heroes typically involve staging. That is, someone in charge has told all involved where to enter and exit the stage, where to sit, where to stand, when to shake hands and pause for a photograph, and whether to pass each other on the left or right as they come and go toward the microphone.

Your staging as a speaker is equally important. Plan where you need to be to use certain audiovisual equipment or to interact with the audience at different points of your presentation. Then move purposefully as you present.

Take your staging to the next level by understanding that staging helps your audience assimilate your information, data, or ideas. If your audience members were *reading* your content rather than hearing it, they would receive transition cues from the page. For example, three separate headings on the page would signal to them that you had three key points or topics. If you had four bullet points under one of those headings, the reader would know you had four supporting details to explain that key topic. White space on the page would provide the reader with a chance to pause and take a breath.

But listeners have none of those cues. If you stand in one spot to deliver the entire talk, everything tends to run together in the listener's mind as if it were in one long paragraph on a page. If, however, you present your first key point standing on the left side of the center front, then move to the right to deliver the second key point, and then stand in the center to make your last key point, you have at least visually etched three "paragraphs" in their mind's eye.

This is simplified staging. It gets more complex from there.

TIP 33: Consider Your Staging as Part of Audience Control

Walking out into the audience shows that you are not afraid to look them in the eye or answer their questions. Be careful about setting up artificial barriers, such as a lectern, table, or raised platform away from the front row of your audience. Physical closeness will lend intimacy to your talk. Unless the lighting or the microphones dictate that you must, do not stand behind a "barrier." Maintain contact with the entire room, and use your entire space—even in a conference room.

Such proximity also helps you keep the attention of audience members. It is difficult to drift off when the speaker is standing three feet from your chair or jotting notes on the chart pad beside you. Physically moving about in your audience's space helps avert certain problems and distractions. For example, just strolling toward their side of the room can quiet a side conversation between two attendees. The talkers feel all eyes following you, and they do not want to be caught in the spotlight talking.

You also can use physical closeness to keep a particular individual from dominating a discussion. In such a situation, casually stroll toward the dominating person and then turn and face the other way to deliver your next point or ask your next question. This physically closes off the dominator, who will likely remain silent until you turn around again.

Your use of physical space should support—rather than detract from—your words.

VOCAL VARIETY: PACE, PITCH, PAUSING, PUNCH, PATTERN, AND PASSION

TIP 34: Add Volume to Increase Authority

In our society, little girls are taught that loud voices are not feminine, whereas little boys learn no such inhibitions. As a result, women often have problems with speaking loudly enough. In today's business arena, wimpy voices get little attention. Consider the extreme. When someone shouts, everyone turns to look—regardless of what's being said. Volume gets attention.

Remember that your voice always sounds louder to you than to anyone else. Take another person's word for it when he or she says you need to speak up. Also remember that your voice is an instrument; it needs to be warmed up, or it will creak and crack at the beginning of your presentation. If you warm up with a high volume, as though projecting to those in the back row, your volume also will improve your vocal quality.

Volume adds energy to your voice; it has the power to command or lose listeners' attention.

TIP 35: Dramatically Increase or Decrease Your Volume to Gain Attention

If you routinely speak loudly, you also can increase attention for a key point by dramatically *decreasing* your volume. Variety grabs attention. If you deliver your entire presentation at the same volume—the perfect volume throughout a half-hour talk—then, by definition, it has become imperfect because of its sameness. After awhile, that volume becomes only background noise.

Consider the effect of a TV playing in the background at home. If you routinely turn it on the moment you walk in the door—whether or not you are watching it—chances are that after a few minutes you mentally tune it out. The sound blends into the other noises of the home or neighborhood—dogs barking, babies crying, blenders swirling, or bathtubs draining. However, if someone comes into the room and turns the TV off or switches the channel, the sudden silence or change in volume gets your attention, right?

The same is true of a speaker. It is the variety of ups and downs that continually invites the audience to reconnect.

TIP 36: Breathe Deeply to Improve Voice Quality

As you breathe, take in enough air so that you are able to complete each sentence briskly rather than having your words drop off at the end. Breath control allows you to stress the most important words and downplay the least important ones. To make sure you take enough air to control your voice, breathe from the diaphragm. Place your hand underneath your rib cage and feel your diaphragm as it moves up and down to allow your lungs to fill. If you cannot feel your diaphragm move up and down, then chances are that you are not breathing deeply enough to control your voice properly. If you are standing and breathing from your diaphragm, your shoulders should not rise.

The deeper you breathe, generally the better you will sound.

TIP 37: Lower Your Pitch to Increase Authority

Pitch, the measurement of the "highness" or "lowness" of your voice, is determined largely by the amount of tension in the vocal cords. When you are under stress, you may sound high-pitched; when you are relaxed and confident, you will have a naturally lower pitch.

Authoritative vocal tones are low and calm, not high and tense. Inflection is a pitch change—from "Stop!" screeched at an assailant to the haughty "Please stop" directed at a stranger using your department's copy machine. You can lower your pitch to some degree by practicing scales (as singers do, dropping the voice with each word) and by breathing more deeply to relax your vocal cords.

Remember that a lower pitch conveys power, authority, and confidence, whereas a high pitch conveys insecurity and nervousness.

TIP 38: Identify Vocal Qualities That May Detract from an Overall Positive Impression

Vocal *quality* refers to such characteristics as a breathy sound, a tense harshness, hoarseness, nasal tones, or a deep, resonant, solemn sound. Vocal quality is also measured by weaknesses such as slurring of words, over- or underarticulating certain sounds or accents, and so forth. You can correct some of these yourself simply by awareness; others may require the help of a voice coach.

TIP 39: Articulate

Remember not to drop final syllables (say *eating* versus *eatin'*), and give full value to all sounds so that words do not run together in a mumble-jumble. Speakers seem to "eat their words" particularly when they get in a hurry to finish a point and their brain runs ahead of their tongue. You may want to warm up with a few tongue twisters you learned back on the playground. Audiences tend to make snap judgments about education based on enunciation.

TIP 40: Put a Smile in Your Tone When Appropriate

Nervous speakers often get so caught up in presenting content that they sound and look much too serious for the occasion. I have seen presenters explain the procedures for completing an expense report or overview the new wing design for their aircraft as though they were delivering a eulogy. Of course, if your topic is a serious one, you may not want to look as though you are announcing a new bonus plan. But do take care that a "serious" tone does not come across as an angry one. Match tone to content.

TIP 41: Vary Your Pace According to Your Purpose

Pace refers to speaking rate—either slow or fast. Neither extreme is right or wrong, but knowing the pros and cons of each will help you determine the effect you want. A fast rate shows excitement and energy and commands listeners' attention so that they do not miss what you say. If you speak too quickly, however, your audience may have trouble understanding your words.

Use a slow speaking rate to add drama, emphasize key points, and give listeners time to reflect on what you are saying. Speaking too slowly, however, may cause listeners' minds to wander or convey the impression that you do not know what is coming next or do not have much information to give. Because people are capable of listening four to six times faster than most people speak, a slow speed may lose your audience entirely.

Again, variety is the key. When presenting serious information, speak a bit slower; for a humorous story, a bit faster. For large audiences, speak slowly enough for your sound and movements to create an impact on those in the back row. For smaller, intimate groups, speed up a little. For example, try

- A slow, resonant, and precise articulation of fourth-quarter profits followed by a speedy, succinct summary

- A quickly delivered rah-rah for the sales team followed by a slow, sincere thank-you for their efforts

TIP 42: Use Silences to Underscore Your Meaning

To put the final polish on your vocal techniques, remember to use silences. Do *not* be afraid of them. Silences do not signal a memory lapse. On the contrary. Used effectively, they interpret your meaning. They say to the audience, "Now just stop and think about that" or "Get ready for this next point—it's important." Silences also give your audience breathing room between ideas.

If you are trying to steer your audience members toward introspection, ask a question and then pause, giving them a chance to formulate their own answers before you share yours. Speeches without pauses cause ideas to run together and make it difficult for listeners to distinguish between major and minor ideas.

TIP 43: Prevent Problems with Your Voice Before
They Happen

Do not wait until you become hoarse to try to take care of your voice if you give frequent presentations. Avoid cold liquids that make your vocal cords contract. Instead, choose beverages at room temperature. And avoid dairy products before you speak, which have the effect of producing "cotton mouth."

Keep in mind that your voice is the medium of your message. While necessary for delivery, it should not call attention to itself. If any of these aspects—volume, pitch, quality, or pace—direct listeners' attention away from your message, your voice has become a liability rather than an asset.

MOVEMENT AND ENERGY TRANSLATED TO PURPOSE

TIP 44: Imagine Yourself as a Light Bulb

The late Hal Persons, personal friend and well-known acting coach who trained Jack Lemmon, among other movie stars, introduced me to this analogy when we occasionally worked together to teach communication skills at IBM. Hal would just as often critique a movie star as a system engineer with this comment: "Hey, you're burning at about 35 watts." Then he would coax them into a more energetic presentation style with this light-bulb imagery: "You've got to push energy to your audience. Otherwise, they're going to go to sleep on you. I want you to push energy out through the pores of your skin. Assume you're at 35 watts now, and I want to see you explain this software application at 60 watts." They would do 60 seconds more. "Stop, stop." He would yell. "Okay, maybe you're at 50 watts. Let's take it to 70 watts." And the systems engineer would start again. "Okay. That was better." He would turn to the rest of the group and say, "So what was that? 70 watts? 75 watts?"

And the presenter's peers would chime in with encouragement as they saw more energy. What exactly were they seeing happen differently? Typically, the speaker's voice grew louder. More inflection on key points. Movement around the room. Spontaneous gestures. And none of this activity was by any specific direction on Hal's part.

It all resulted from energy. And energy resulted from the light-bulb analogy. When you feel trapped in a low-energy mood or locked into that mindset permanently, break out by considering the light bulb.

POISE, POMP, AND CIRCUMSTANCE

TIP 45: Take Stage

I am not talking about the "changing of the guard" at Buckingham Palace, but think of your audience members as people visiting an amusement park and yourself as the Ferris wheel operator. The audience members have climbed into their seats and are waiting for you to flip the switch and send them swirling. If you do not, they will just sit there, mentally and physically frustrated.

Likewise, when you are speaking to a group, the power or intensity you exhibit in your delivery is the voltage the audience needs. They anticipate it and respond to it. There should be no doubt that you have taken control of a meeting, discussion, or presentation.

Your audience may be watching you even before you take the stage. While you are waiting for your time in the limelight, do not fidget with your clothes, pat your hair into place, shuffle through your notes, or reorder your visuals. Such activity connotes a lack of interest in and respect for the current proceedings, as if you are merely waiting for the most important event—your talk—to begin.

So how do you command attention from the start of your presentation? With your posture, body language, movement toward the front of the group, and opening remarks.

If an introducer is particularly flowery, avoid the eyes of the audience and simply smile as if acknowledging that the words are a little too much. Your first eye contact with the audience should be when you stand up to face them.

Approach the presentation area with deliberate, purposeful steps, not as though you were being dragged forward against your will. Stand with your weight evenly on both feet, not slumped to the side or leaning against a table or lectern. Take a moment to get your bearings. Place any notes or visuals in front of you. Make any necessary adjustments to any equipment you plan to use. Then look out at your audience and pause. Greet them, and then respond to the introduction, acknowledge the occasion, or simply begin your presentation.

These opening few seconds are critical. This is when your audience takes stock of you and decides whether you are worth listening to. By the time you open your mouth, half your opportunity to make a good impression is already gone.

Taking stage also includes your opening remarks—those made before your prepared presentation material. For example, you might acknowledge your introduction or the occasion. Or you might compliment the audience or verify their comfort before beginning. Above all, avoid opening clichés that mark you as insincere, a lazy thinker, or both.

Instead of relying on stale clichés, start fresh. Say what's on your mind—sincerely. "Thank you for that introduction" is adequate and appropriate on occasion. You may add a comment about why you were asked to speak, compliment the audience, mention the importance of the subject matter, or comment on your state of mind or mood and how it relates to the occasion, subject, or audience. If you are particularly quick-witted, you may refer to some incident, joke, or occurrence from earlier in the program that ties into your introductory remarks. Such an impromptu delivery will impress your audience with your wit, freshness, and willingness to depart from "scripted" lines.

Take charge completely with your posture, body language, eye contact, vocal tone, and fresh comments. Do not be tentative. Project an attitude of anticipation and eagerness. Look confident. Let the audience know that you have come to deliver value and are about to unleash a slew of benefits if they will just listen up.

TIP 46: Talk Rather Than Read

The reason we have so many sluggish speeches is that many speakers read to their audiences—often something never meant to be read aloud. The differences in spoken and written communication are enormous. For one thing, readers can reread a document if they do not understand it the first time; in spoken communication, the listener has only one chance to understand. A reader can stop, put the document aside, and consult a reference book for the meaning of a word. A listener cannot. A reader can reread and untangle a long sentence. A listener cannot. A reader can brush up on key points by reviewing the structure of the document. A listener cannot review unless the speaker repeats key points and provides visuals.

Simply being aware of the differences between written and spoken language will make you more conscious of what it takes to get across a complex concept to an audience—far more than reading a published paper to them.

TIP 47: Use Simple Words

The most predictable effect of using words that your audience does not understand is that they will stop listening. Or worse, they will feel angry or insulted, assuming that you are trying to impress them or make them feel ignorant or that you did not care enough to find out in advance how much they know about your subject. And all these reactions are detrimental to your purposes.

We will make no distinction between the terrorists and the nations who harbor them.
—*George W. Bush, Jr.*

We can do no great things—only small things with great love.
—*Mother Teresa*

Give me liberty or give me death.
—*Patrick Henry*

I have a dream.
—*Martin Luther King*

Ask not what your country can do for you; ask what you can do for your country.
—*John F. Kennedy*

I'd like to teach the world to sing in perfect harmony.
—*lyric of popular song*

Haste makes waste.
—*familiar saying*

We have nothing to fear but fear itself.
—*Franklin D. Roosevelt*

I am the Way, the Truth, and the Life.
—*Jesus Christ*

Open this gate... Tear down this wall.
—*Ronald Reagan*

It takes a village.
—*Hillary Clinton*

It's the real thing.
—*Coca-Cola ad*

The simple word creates impact.

Big words are not necessarily a sign of intelligence. The ability to make a complex subject understandable to the layperson is the mark of an effective communicator. The simple word creates impact.

TIP 48: Choose the Familiar Word Over the Unfamiliar

Use *unusual* instead of *anomalous, many* instead of *myriad, displeased* instead of *chagrined, cuts* instead of *lacerations, mysterious* instead of *esoteric, everpresent* instead of *ubiquitous.*

TIP 49: Choose the Specific Word Over the General

Use *warehouse* instead of *facility, Chevy truck* instead of *vehicle, damaged keyboards* rather than *unsalable merchandise.* Prefer "The supplier refuses to offer a volume discount" to "The supplier is uncooperative."

TIP 50: Choose the Short Word Over the Long

Prefer *use* instead of *utilize, change* instead of *modification, limits* rather than *parameters.* As Mark Twain once put it, "I never write 'metropolis' for seven cents, because I can get the same money for 'city.' I never write 'policeman,' because I can get the same price for 'cop.'" Do not let your education prevent you from being an effective communicator. A large vocabulary comes in handy to understand someone else or to select just the right word to convey your message. But do not show it off and confuse your audience.

TIP 51: Choose Short Sentences Over Long Ones

Long sentences lose listeners. Short ones are clearer and easier to deliver with a normal breathing rhythm. With written documents, readers can reread when they miss a point. With presentations, however, listeners do not have this option. Spoken sentences must be much shorter than written ones. The reason for so many deadly speeches is that sometimes presenters actually try to "speak" their written papers (such as those prepared from academic research or project reports to management).

TIP 52: Verify Pronunciation or Stay Clear of Routinely Troublesome Words

Someone in an audience once corrected my pronunciation of *subsidence* in such an embarrassing way that I will never mispronounce it again. Lyndon Johnson's speechwriters avoided words he found difficult to say, and I have found this to be the best solution for myself. In taping an audio series with Nightingale-Conant, I learned that I simply cannot pronounce the word *error;* so I remember to say *mistake* instead.

A colleague of mine pronounced the word *relevant* as "revelant" (a common mispronunciation) over and over during an important customer briefing. Her boss, sitting in on the meeting, made note of the error and corrected her afterward, but not in time to prevent the smirks of the customers my colleague had hoped to impress. Using a simpler, more familiar word is always preferable to using one that you mumble, muffle, slur, or overarticulate due to anxiety about getting it right.

TIP 53: Use Specific, Vivid Language

Use graphic "picture" words that enable audiences to see and feel. Not "an angry individual" but "a yelling, freckle-faced teenager." Not "an orderly process" but "a print run of 10,000 copies without a single skipped page or ink smudge in the margins." Not "a growing concern to our profitability" but "in 6 months we'll be in the red by $90,000." Not "we're hoping for increased productivity" but "we expect to double the number of calls our technicians can handle per hour."

TIP 54: Use the "You" Approach

Focus on your audience members as if talking to them individually. Not "Commonly acknowledged among internists, . . ." but "As you are probably aware . . ." Not "If there seems to be a synergy among the two entities and they agree to cooperate" but "If we agree to work together . . ."

When using an illustration, make it come alive by putting your listeners in the center of the action: Not "The typical auditor feels rebuffed when making visits to our plant sites" but "Imagine yourself as an auditor assigned to visit one of our plant sites. What reception would you expect from the manager if you . . . ?"

TIP 55: Omit Clichés of the Occasion

Avoid the tired, overused phrases that sound as though they were lifted from a procedures book on corporate presentations: "proposing solutions," "discovering synergies," "facing an important challenge." Likewise, these platitudes can be shoved into you "inactive" files: "people are our greatest asset," "we welcome the opportunity," "we must forge ahead," "we are only as good as the decisions we make," "he fought a hard fight." Such expressions either reflect lazy thinking or sound out of place and dramatic in describing everyday situations.

TIP 56: Use Colloquialisms and Slang When Appropriate

Just as we dress differently on different occasions, we speak in ways that create identification with a particular audience. "He informed us of his decision about the downsizing" is formal. "He laid it on the line about our jobs" is informal. Your use of formal or informal expressions should match both the topic and the audience.

TIP 57: Avoid Poor Grammar

Proper grammar is still the mark of education in our society. Watch for incorrect use of pronouns, such as "John and him went on the plant tour" or "You can give the report to Cary or myself." Watch for misplaced adjectives when adverbs are called for, such as "He did good" when you mean "He did well." Be careful about subject-verb agreement, such as "He don't have the proper identification" when you mean "He doesn't have the proper identification."

If you're feeling a little panicky about this issue, consider reviewing a good grammar text. If I may sneak in a brief commercial here, mine is called *Good Grief, Good Grammar*. It starts with the basics, adds a little humor, and highlights the tips most appropriate for businesspeople.

TIP 58: Don't "Let Down" for Sit-Down Presentations

In a business setting, particularly during sales calls, you may make presentations to only one person or two or three seated around a decision maker's desk. Although there is no correlation between audience size and importance of the outcome, consider several issues in light of the setting.

First of all, consider the group's expectations. Do not assume that because the audience is small, its members do not expect a formal presentation—visuals and the works.

Second, because you are seated around a desk or table—at eye level with the group—you must convey your enthusiasm, assertiveness, and authority at "half mast," through your facial expressions, posture, and voice. Sitting down may tempt you to slouch, but don't. Sit comfortably erect, leaning slightly forward in your chair to show attentiveness and enthusiasm for your subject. Sit back in your chair to convey openness to questions.

Position yourself to maintain eye contact with everyone in the room. Do not get stuck between two listeners so that you have to turn your head back and forth with each point, as though you are watching a game of table tennis. If possible, remove any physical obstacles that block vision or create "distance" between you and your audience—such as a shelf that juts out from the wall or a table or desk plant you must dodge to make eye contact. If the setup is not conducive to the business at hand, request a change: "Do you mind if I move over to this side of the room so that these shelves do not block our view?"

After deciding where and how to seat yourself while addressing your small group, be sure your visuals will be positioned so that your audience can see them readily. Remember, your audience, not you, needs to be able to read them. A glance—even an upside-down one—at your visual should be all you need to cue you to your next point.

Sitting down or standing up—decisions count either way.

TIP 59: Involve Your Audience in a Variety of Ways

Audience involvement may take the form of an opinion poll with a show of hands, a volunteer for a demonstration, a quiz, an anecdote about an audience member, or a simple question—rhetorical or otherwise. Even in such formal situations as State-of-the-Union addresses delivered before Congress, the President often refers to people in the audience, asking them to stand and be recognized as he tells their story.

In brief, 30-second TV commercials, a corporate spokesperson looks right into the camera with this audience-involvement technique, the rhetorical question: "Whom do *you* trust to manage *your* retirement fund?" or "Do you know how much money the lobbyists gave your congressional representative last year?" or "Do you know how much we spent studying *X* topic last year?"

This strategy is so important with today's audiences that I have devoted an entire chapter to such techniques—Chapter 11. Never underestimate the power of involving your audience.

TIP 60: End with Impact

Don't whimper to a close. We have all witnessed speakers who mumbled their last lines while shuffling their notes and shutting down their laptops. "I guess that's about all I have." (Awkward pause.) "Any questions?" they add as an afterthought, never making eye contact to welcome any. Then they slink back to their seats, averting their eyes until someone else assumes control of the meeting.

You can do much better than this. To end with impact, leave your audience with a dramatic closing line (tips on this in Chapter 4). Then stop when you are finished. Now this may sound like stating the obvious, but not all presenters do. Some have developed the bad habit of delivering their strong, prepared closing and then reexplaining, adding, and clarifying points, ultimately ending on an anticlimactic note. Abe Lincoln once remarked of such a speaker, "He can compress the most words into the smallest idea of any man I ever met."

To say more than needs to be said is a great mistake. Remember that the Lord's Prayer is only 71 words long, the Ten Commandments are 297 words long, and the Gettysburg Address (the most quoted speech in history) is only 271 words long. In my experience, and probably in yours, those with the most significant message usually deliver it in the fewest words.

When your idea runs its course, simply stop. Add nothing. Do not mumble. Pause for one last look at your audience, confident that they will agree with what you have just said. Then return to your seat in the same deliberate, purposeful way you approached the group.

4
Creating Your Content, Organizing Your Information, Polishing Your Points

A speech without a specific purpose is like a journey without a destination.
RALPH C. SMEDLEY

In order to speak short upon any subject, think long.
H. H. BRACKENRIDGE

In some respects a speech is like a love affair. Any fool can start one, but to end it requires considerable skill.
LORD MANCROFT

Banality is a symptom of non-communication. Men hide behind their clichés.
EUGENE IONESCO

Pun: The lowest form of humor, unless you thought of it first.
UNKNOWN

Wit ought to be a glorious treat, like caviar. Never spread it about like marmalade.
NOEL COWARD

Your preparation for a presentation typically will involve these key steps. That preparation may take only a few minutes or many weeks depending on the length of your talk, how well you already know your topic, and how high the stakes are that you "get it right."

- Determine your purpose.
- Analyze your audience.
- Research and gather your information.
- Compose a one-sentence or one-paragraph overview of your main message to serve as a roadmap.
- Organize your ideas and information with an idea wheel.
- Create a detailed outline, including an attention-getting opening, smooth transitions, a strong closing, and all the finishing touches that make your presentation colorful.
- Write a first draft of a script (occasionally).
- Edit and polish your content.
- Prepare any supporting visuals.
- Anticipate questions and prepare your answers.
- Prepare notes or an outline for delivery.
- Practice your speech using your notes or outline.
- Prepare a key-word outline for delivery.
- Destroy your script, notes, or complete outline and use your key-word outline to deliver your presentation to your audience.

How necessary is this preparation? Why not just "wing it," as the less prepared say?

Not unlike Olympic athletes training for the big event, speakers must do a great deal of work developing their presentations before appearing in front of a group. The need to know where you are going—and how to get there—is just as great in communication as in the sports arena.

YOUR PURPOSE

TIP 61: Determine Your Purpose Before You Do *Anything* Else

Presenters typically have one or more of these five basic purposes: to inform, to persuade, to inspire and motivate, to instruct, or to entertain.

To inform. "Absenteeism cost our company $2 million last year, and we predict an increase of 30 percent in the coming year."

To inform: Key message _____
    Fact 1 _____
    Fact 2 _____

To persuade: Key message/action wanted _____
    Reason 1 _____
    Reason 2 _____

To inspire/motivate: Key message _____
    Illustration or fact 1 _____
    Illustration or fact 2 _____

To instruct: Key concept _____
    Illustration, fact, or information A _____
    Illustration, fact, or information B _____

To entertain: Key point _____
    Anecdote or illustration 1 _____
    Anecdote or illustration 2 _____

Determine your purpose before you build your structure.

To persuade. "Absenteeism cost our company too much. Therefore, I'm proposing that we begin health-awareness programs that reduce stress, prevent disease, and increase overall fitness. Why? Because healthier employees miss less work and are more productive."

To inspire/motivate. "Our average employee misses fewer than 1.2 days per year for health-related reasons. We commend you for your progressive attitude about proper nutrition, exercise, and overall fitness. We plan to offer a $500 bonus to every employee with a perfect attendance record over the next year."

To instruct. "I'd like to suggest three ways to help you reduce job-induced stress. Then we'll discuss the essentials of proper diet."

To entertain. "Trying to maintain good health when you're basically a lazy person can be time-consuming. It took me a week just to map out a jogging trail along my driveway. In fact, a friend of mine recently said it took him four days to get his bicycle greased because. . . ."

You may decide to fine-tune your overview message to fit one of these categories. Then select your supporting facts, reasons, illustrations, or anecdotes.

**Never underestimate the importance
of understanding the mission!**

Within these broad categorical purposes, you typically will have to get more specific to be successful. For example, if you plan to inform a group, you certainly cannot count on their remembering your complete half hour's presentation of planned budget cuts. Instead, focus on the two or three key points that you want them to walk away with.

The purpose sets up the goal posts.

TIP 62: To Sharpen Your Focus on Your Purpose, Ask "Why Me?"

Why have you been selected to present this information or message? What specific qualities or credentials do you have? Pinpointing your unique qualifications will provide a major clue about the strengths only you can bring to the talk. For example, were you particularly close to a business associate so that you can add emotional depth to his farewell address? As the specialist who did the research on a project, can you answer questions more authoritatively than anyone else? Do you have access to certain data that no one else has? Have others with the same expertise been passed over, and have you been invited to speak because of your humorous approach? Are you a recognized authority for a certain viewpoint? Will the audience expect to hear your personal experiences about already accepted ideas?

TIP 63: To Complete the Focus on Your Purpose, Ask "Why Them?"

Why has this particular group assembled to hear you? Have their bosses, clients, suppliers, or spouses requested that they attend? Do they have a personal interest in you? Do they have an interest in the subject? Do they want to hear what you have to say so that they can contradict you and subvert your efforts and ideas? Did they come to hear someone else, and you happened to be on the program? Is this their monthly organizational meeting, and they are expected to show up? Honest answers to these questions can help you choose appropriate opening remarks, the right tone, and the best order for presenting your ideas.

TIP 64: Imagine You Were Going to Be Forced to Measure and Report on Your Success

Let's go back to the previous example about informing your group on planned budget cuts. If the group members can recall those points a week later, you have achieved your purpose to inform; if they cannot, you have not been successful.

If your purpose is to instruct a group of employees on taking credit-card applications over the phone, then you can measure whether you achieved that purpose fairly easily: Can they complete the applications without error?

If your purpose is to motivate them to adopt a healthier lifestyle, you can determine your success by the action they take: increased exercise, reduced stress, more nutritious, healthier meals, and so forth.

Thinking of the pressure of having to measure and report on your specific success—what your audience members do or do not remember, do or do not do, understand or do not understand—will lead you to focus on the essentials of your content.

And this focus ultimately helps you to weed out the "nice to include" ideas and information from the "must include" ideas and information—a particularly helpful practice when you know a lot about your topic and have less time than you would like to share it.

Visualize yourself measuring and reporting on your results with your audience, and sort and sift your information accordingly.

YOUR AUDIENCE ANALYSIS

TIP 65: Profile Your Audience with an Extensive Questionnaire

Although you will not find this doable or desirable on every occasion, gathering background information can be enormously helpful. And most of the time you do not even know *how* it will help you until after you collect the data. For starters, find answers to these key questions:

- What is the age, sex, race, religion, or political bent of the audience members?
- What is the proportion of men to women?
- What is their educational background?
- What is their occupation?
- Is their work experience technical or nontechnical?
- What is their income level?
- What do their individual lifestyles have in common?
- What organizations do they belong to?
- What is their individual motivation for hearing the presentation?
- What are some of the potential uses for your information?

- What are their prejudices and biases about this subject?
- What is their knowledge of the subject?
- What are their opinions about the organization you represent?
- What are their current problems or challenges?
- What are their goals and wants?
- Are they decision makers? Influencers? Implementers?
- What are the significant events related to this meeting, department, corporation, city, or organization?
- Are there any taboo subjects or issues?
- Will they appreciate humor, or is this a solemn occasion?
- What is their style of learning—seeing, hearing, doing? How much interactivity do they typically have in similar sessions?
- How do they feel about attending this presentation? Passive? Inconvenienced? Competitive with you, the speaker, or each other? Unified with you, the speaker, and others in the audience? Manipulated for having to attend or participate in any way? Resistant to your ideas and philosophy? Afraid they will not understand what you are saying? Challenged to adopt your ideas? Eager to apply your information? Uncomfortable with the setting?
- How many people will be in the audience? (This will determine your use of visuals, room arrangement, and interaction possibilities.)
- What is the layout of the room? Can it be altered?
- Will food and/or beverages be served before, during, or after the presentation?
- How will attendees be dressed?
- What topics have other speakers on the program (or in past programs) addressed? What was the audience reaction?
- Is there a meeting theme? If so, what is it?
- Will there be a formal question-and-answer period?
- Will special VIPs, guests, or the press be present?

TIP 66: Interview Your Key Contacts to Gather "Inside Information"

Start with the person who invited you to make the presentation, and be specific. Instead of asking, "Could you tell me a little about the group?" ask, "What details can you give me that will help me customize my comments to the unique needs and characteristics of the audience?" Ask about written evaluations or hearsay and anecdotal comments about the group's reactions to past meetings or to industry news. If necessary, be ready with your written list of questions.

Don't stop there, however. I have often discovered that those who *plan* meetings sometimes know very little about the interests and knowledge of those who actually will *attend* the meeting. Planners tend to differ from audience members, too, in their view of the meeting's purpose.

If you're presenting your proposal to a customer, ask your immediate contact the same kinds of questions: How many will attend my presentation? Are these engineers more interested in the software applications or the hardware? Have you compared our equipment with other products on the market? What were your reservations about our competitors' products? What are the three most serious problems your engineers face on this project? What is your time frame for making a purchase decision?

After you talk to those in charge of the program or presentation, go to the next level of interviewees—actual or prospective audience members. Phone a select few ahead of time, survey all potential attendees with a formal questionnaire, or stand at the door and chat with individuals as they arrive. Even this last-minute data collection is better than none at all. With little or no preparation time and in light of new information gained about your audience's interests, you can decide to add or delete a point, spend three minutes longer on point A and three minutes less on point B, or substitute illustration C for illustration D to make the same point more relevant to the audience's experience.

TIP 67: Research Published Information About the Group

Other sources for general information include literature published by the group or offered by its organization: Web site pages, general brochures, sales and marketing literature, product catalogs, annual reports, histories of the organization, journal articles published by its members in industry or business publications, and copies of past program bulletins and evaluations.

TIP 68: Group Your Audience into Categories and Determine How to Win Them Over

After researching your audience, your next step is to get specific about what it will take to meet or exceed their expectations. It may help to group them in categories such as these:

The fans. These audience members are interested in your topic and looking for ways they can support your key message. What opportunity can you give them to speak up and help you sell your idea to the rest of the group? What data or information can you provide to help them pass along the information they already have on the subject?

The undecided but open. These audience members will be attentive. What depth and authority do they need to step over the line?

The hostile. These attendees have an opposing mission and will be ready to challenge whatever you say. They may or may not communicate their concerns or ask questions. They may or may not show interest openly. What can you do to minimize their impact on the rest of the group?

The bored. These people are trapped in your presentation for whatever reason. They may sit quietly and not cause trouble or may ask questions or raise issues to alleviate their boredom. They may unknowingly make your job more difficult or distract others from the action you want. What can you do to involve them in a positive rather than negative way?

TIP 69: Never Underestimate the Importance of Customizing

You cannot develop a boilerplate presentation and expect it to fit all audiences anymore than your parents can pick out your prom dress or tux on the day of your birth. Chances that it will fit are slim. Certainly once you put effort into preparing a presentation—let's say to introduce a new marketing campaign throughout your organization—you will want to be able to use that basic information for all groups of employees. But never expect that you can use that presentation *verbatim*. You will need to shape and reshape it to make sure the illustrations, data, examples, word choice, and tone are all appropriate to each specific group. This is why extemporaneous speaking still requires humans!

TIP 70: Remember That Every Audience Takes on a Life and Personality of Its Own

Keep in mind that every audience has a life and personality of its own. A group's unique chemistry can turn individuals into a supportive, challenged audience that hangs on your every word. Or the combination of personalities can make the majority conform to the passive or negative reaction of a few leaders. Despite the phenomenon of group synergy, which remains a mystery until you begin speaking, do everything possible to learn all you can about the group in advance. Then be "present" and spontaneous enough to "go with the flow" as you read your audience and the current situation.

YOUR TOPIC RESEARCH

TIP 71: Keep an Ongoing Collection of "Snippets" on Your Topics of Interest or Specialization

Even if you are not a professional speaker on the lecture circuit, you undoubtedly have personal and professional interests in certain subjects. Keep ongoing tidbits that might be useful to you later in a presentation about these subjects or your industry: illustrations, quotations, statistics, survey results, research summaries, and anecdotes. Jot the source and date in the margin of each clipping, and toss it into the appropriate paper file. Or scan or record the information in your computer research database.

For years I have kept such an assorted collection on my topics of interest in life balance and communication—most of them tossed into about 15 different paper files labeled according to my most frequently requested aspects of communication. Then several years ago I switched over to a massive computer database to store all the research. I assure you, however, that either system will work. The best system is the one that you will *use* consistently.

TIP 72: Search the Web Efficiently

Lack of information is rarely the problem—the issue is culling through the massive amounts of information available at the click of a mouse to find the perfect fact, statistic, or quotation. You will find some of the best listings of experts on a variety of topics and industries in three primary ways on the Web: (1) Examine various speaker bureau Web sites, which list thousands of the world's most renowned authors, consultants, sports figures, politicians, and government and business leaders. (2) Once you have the names of these experts, you can interview them or find their research in published books, newsletters, and articles, often available on their individual Web sites. (3) Universities provide other experts typically involved in ongoing research.

Here are additional Web sites you may find useful:

www.ipl.org. Almanacs, calendars, dictionaries, quotations, phone numbers and addresses, biographies, style and writing guides

www.firstgov.gov. Information, services, and resources from the U.S. government *www.bls.gov.* U.S. Department of Labor statistics

www.access.gpo.gov. Online U.S. government manual published every two years that includes brief histories and current programs for agencies associated with all areas of the government and the military; also contains listings for independent establishments, government corporations, boards, commissions and committees, and quasi-official agencies

www.associationcentral.com. Association-related information, products, and services showcase for associations (Then the specific associations can lead you to their industry-specific information.)

www.ipl.org/div/aon/. Guide to Web sites of prominent organizations and associations

http://infomine.ucr.edu. 23,000 searchable, academically valuable resources

www.invisibleweb.com. Directory of over 10,000 databases, archives, and search engines that traditional search engines do not typically access

www.ask.com (Ask Jeeves). General information

www.refdesk.com. General information

www.ceoexpress.com. General business information of interest to executives

www.completeplanet.com. 103,000 searchable databases and specialty search engines

TIP 73: Identify Who Else Has a "Need to Know" to Locate Hard-to-Find Information

For hard-to-find information, ask yourself who else would be most likely to want to know certain facts, statistics, or trends. If you need to know the average woman's shoe size, who else would likely need to know this information and have already researched it? Shoe manufacturers? Retail shoe or department stores? If you need to know how many parking spaces the average dentist provides for clients, who should you consult? Commercial developers? Strip-mall building managers? Dental clinic administrators? If you need to know the number of abortions performed in the United States last year, would you call the Department of Health and Human Services? The local abortion clinic? Local antiabortion agencies? A school counselor?

Call a local university professor for an expert opinion on a technical subject. A corporate public relations office can help with quotations from the chief executive officer (CEO) or financials published in the company's annual report. A publisher can put you in touch with a book's author for a fresh quotation on a current event. Whatever your subject or need, some expert will know or be willing to offer a fresh perspective.

Also don't overlook the wealth of information at your disposal through a phone call to your local public or university librarian. Libraries have resources that the Internet does not. Many libraries offer a reference desk with staff who specialize and delight in finding hard-to-locate information for you—even at odd hours of the day or night. Researchers, armed with a master's degree in library science or in information services, can ferret out sources, facts, and data you never dreamed existed and call you back within minutes to give you just the exact detail to make your talk authoritative.

TIP 74: Avoid Common Research Pitfalls

The Internet has made researching easy. By the same token, the Internet has made researching *precisely* more difficult. Mistakes proliferate around the globe at the speed of a click. So keep the following guidelines in mind:

- Be wary about facts for which no source is listed—electronically, in print, on TV. If your whole point rests on a certain fact, check more than one source to validate it.

- Attribute quotations correctly. While doing research for a previous book, I found a particular Pascal quotation (true source as verified by a Pascal scholar at the University of California who referred me to the original Pascal source document) attributed to no fewer than four other authors—Teddy Roosevelt, Andrew Jackson, Mark Twain, and Winston Churchill. Reference books are highly reliable; memories are not.

- Do not use an exceptional situation to prove your key point.

- Avoid sweeping generalizations of unsupported opinions.

- Do not take things out of context. The temptation may be great to lift an attention-getting passage or comment from a university professor, an author, or another recognized expert and then flesh it out with your own assumptions. It is quite embarrassing, however, when someone in your audience points out that the expert you quoted actually supports the opposing idea.

- State your assumptions up front.

- Consider the validity of other positions on an issue; even if you do not present the opposing views, doing so will produce a more thorough and objective analysis of the subject.

Sound like a lot of work? It is time-consuming to double-check sources, facts, and so forth. But your responsibilities include putting in the time needed to ensure credibility. As a speaker, you are morally obligated to present the truth, without deception. A second incentive for verifying your information is to avoid the embarrassment of having an audience member call your error to light.

TIP 75: Do Not Overlook Personal Experience— Yours or That of Others—as You "Research"

Examine your background for anecdotes, overheard conversations, reactions to problems, and feelings and moods that underscore the key points of your presentation. Many people keep a journal of memorable experiences, conversations, or happenings they have witnessed or been part of. You never know when such an incident will be the exact illustration you need to make your point and win audience identification.

Next, ask friends, acquaintances, and coworkers for similar anecdotes or personal experiences. You will be surprised at how many illustrations you can gather to reinforce your points just by mentioning your subject over lunch or during casual conversations.

YOUR STRUCTURE: MOVING BEYOND FIRST, SECOND, THIRD . . .

TIP 76: Compose a Brief Overview

This one-paragraph overview serves as your roadmap. It marries your message to your audience with the expectation of listeners following your presentation. For example:

> Our record-storage center has reached capacity. This warehouse space, which costs us approximately $90,000 annually, houses primarily useless information. I recommend that we revise our record-retention schedules, purge our current files, terminate our lease on the warehouse site, and begin a paperwork-reduction campaign. Within three years we can reduce our paperwork costs by an estimated $1.8 million. I need your approval to implement these changes.

With such a comprehensive yet focused roadmap at the beginning, your presentation practically composes itself. In the preceding example, the key supporting points are obvious: (1) current situation of waste and cost, (2) record-retention schedules—current and proposed, (3) how-tos of purging current files, (4) details of terminating the warehouse lease, (5) steps, costs, and how-tos of paperwork-reduction campaign, (6) estimation of savings, and (7) approval needed.

Composing a succinct overview is the single most important thing you can do to ensure an effective presentation. You need a speech theme or point of view like a product needs a slogan. It is a rallying call. Half your preparation is done at this point.

TIP 77: Narrow Your Ideas to a Few Key Points

Contrary to what you may think, you are likely to struggle more with narrowing your ideas to a few good points than with generating enough ideas to support your general message. For most business occasions, your key points are pretty well defined by the purpose of the meeting.

Just remember that in this era of 30-second commercials, one-sentence newspaper updates, 8-line "e-zines," 15-word cell-phone text messages, 200-word magazine articles, 15-minute oil changes, 20-minute pizza deliveries, and 1-hour photos, your audience appreciates brevity. And so do corporate pocketbooks. Figure the salaries of those gathered to hear you, and ask yourself if each of your points is worth $X per minute.

TIP 78: Include an Opening, a Body, and a Closing

Jot down the key points you have in mind to support your message statement. Then list questions your audience is likely to have about the subject. Put these notes aside for a few days, and let your subconscious mull over the ideas. As you come up with subpoints, additional illustrations, and other relevant tidbits, throw them on top of your notes pile. When you are ready to construct a formal outline, go through the pile and sort the items into a logical order (as explained later in this book). Discard anything that does not seem to fit anymore. You are now ready to write a formal outline using these major headings: opening, body, and closing.

TIP 79: Determine the Basic Framework

Your topic generally will lend itself to one of these basic arrangements:

Topical. "We recommend a combination of ways to stay healthy—practice good nutrition, get exercise, reduce stress, and avoid substance abuse."

Most important to least important. "The most important way to stay healthy is to avoid drugs and alcohol. The second is to eat properly. Third is proper exercise."

Problem to solution. "Absenteeism is costing us $2 million annually. Most absences are health-related. We need to teach our employees how to stay healthy and reinforce their efforts through company-sponsored exercise facilities, subsidized meal plans, and substance-abuse counseling."

Chronological. "In 1992, absenteeism cost us $X. In 1997, it cost $Y. In 2002, it cost $Z. This year we predict a 15 percent increase, for a total of $22 million, unless we take immediate action. I suggest that a company-sponsored health-maintenance plan be implemented during the next three years. In the first and second quarters, we could provide. . . . In the second half of the year, we could. . . ."

Comparison/contrast. "Our rate of absenteeism is twice as high as the industry average. And yet our average employee is younger, lives closer to the job, and works shorter hours."

Geographic. "Our absenteeism rate in Atlanta is X because. . . . In Dallas, it's Y because. . . . In Minneapolis, the rate is Z because. . . ."

Spatial/physical form. "In the north wing we could accommodate an indoor walking/running track. In the south wing we could set up a small cafeteria."

Cause to effect/effect to cause. "Employees often work 12-hour days and do not have the time or energy to cook or exercise when they get home. Therefore, they do not take time to prepare nutritious meals or to exercise. Our average employee asks for a transfer every six months due to on-the-job stress. We think this stress is related to short deadlines, malfunctioning equipment, and customer complaints."

Frequency. "Most employee absences are due to respiratory infections, so I want to outline our plans to deal with those problems primarily. The second most commonly reported illness is stomach flu, so I will overview how to handle those cases next. Information on the less frequent absences caused by a heart condition will be summarized briefly in a handout."

Most difficult to least difficult. "Our biggest challenge will be bankrolling the health facilities. Our next biggest challenge will be finding qualified medical advisers."

Objections/answers. "Management's main objection will be the cost. However, studies in companies similar to ours show that health prevention costs much less than absenteeism."

Goal/steps. "Our number one goal is to maintain an average of no more than one absence per employee annually. Here are the three steps necessary to achieve this."

Status quo/change. "We now allow employees 10 days of sick leave each year. Under the new plan, we would provide five days of sick leave but offer a bonus for unused leave."

Feature/benefits. "This exercise bike has a tilt bar that. . . . This feature allows the rider to change positions and exercise different abdominal muscles simply by. . . ."

Procedures. "The first step is to appoint a management committee. The second step is to form a volunteer employee advisory board. This board will then draft policies and submit them to the entire organization."

Narration. "One of our managers, Omar Kopek, noted an increased number of employees out on sick leave following the three stress-filled weeks in the Leola plant. Some of his people reported. . . ."

Description. "The food service will include.... The exercise room will have four rowing machines designed to...."

Your presentation may encompass several of these frameworks. For example, your main framework may be problem to solution, but under your point about proper nutrition, you may mention features of the food facility you want to fund.

This extensive list should help you generate a number of ways to think about your topic. Once you understand the broad range of ways to organize your supporting detail, you probably will generate many more ideas than you will have time to present.

Then, with your overview statement or paragraph (roadmap) and key points plugged into an overall framework, look for anecdotes, statistics, explanations, testimonials, facts, or illustrations to flesh out or further support your points.

TIP 80: Consider This Format for a "Problem to Solution" Presentation

Overview the problem. Recommend the solution. Elaborate on the details of the solution—why and how. Mention briefly other possible solutions that you investigated and rejected. Outline the next steps. Recap the solution and results.

TIP 81: Consider This Format for a "Goal and Steps" Presentation

State the goal in terms that will interest your audience. Overview all steps to the goal. Elaborate on each step separately. Present an action plan with a timeline. Recap the goal.

TIP 82: Consider This Format for a "Budget Justification" Presentation

State the budget request. Summarize the justification or uses for the money. Point out significant decreases and increases from previous periods. Elaborate on key uses or results expected for the budget increases. Mention significant timing issues. Recap your key request and uses.

TIP 83: Consider This Format for a "Product or Service Overview" Presentation

Introduce your product or service. Differentiate your product or service in the marketplace. Overview key benefits or advantages. Overview marketing plans, sales goals, and time lines.

TIP 84: Consider This Format for a "Status Report" Presentation

Overview the key accomplishments or summarize the current status of a project. Highlight the significance of the latest accomplishment or results. Elaborate only on key details—usually the how and why. Overview the next steps briefly. Ask for any necessary approval on next steps.

TIP 85: Generate Details and a Full Outline with an Idea Wheel

The idea wheel lets you capture several hours' worth of ideas in a single view. You can easily use it to give a 10-minute talk on a school fund-raiser or a half-day presentation to a prospect about your organization's financial

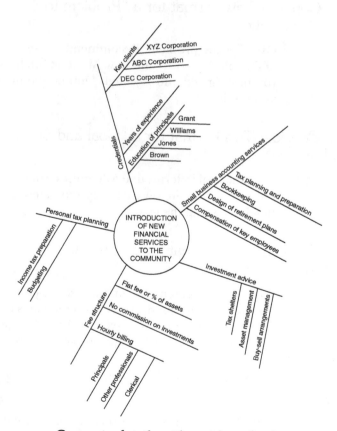

Generate details with an idea wheel.

services. The advantage of keeping the whole structure in front of you is that, at a glance, you know where you have been and where you are going. In fact, when developing a team presentation, you may decide to draw your idea wheel on a flipchart to let your group see the structure of the talk as it evolves.

TIP 86: Determine the Proper Tone

Do you want to be formal? Warm and witty? Light? Humorous? Serious? Informative? Persuasive? Entertaining? This decision will affect your word choice, your anecdotes—even your key points and supporting detail. Discard any information that might contribute to an undesirable tone.

Additionally, to some extent your audience will dictate your tone. When addressing your boss or other superiors, you will make recommendations and suggestions rather than lecture or dictate a course of action. To peers and team members, you will use the "we" approach, providing information and examples, asking for input, and answering questions.

To groups with special interests such as clients or political or social groups, you will focus on their concerns and weed out irrelevant data and illustrations. You will adopt a persuasive tone and offer your opinion, personal experiences, and preferences.

TIP 87: Plan the Overall Timing

You do not want an introduction that runs 10 minutes when your whole speech lasts only 20 minutes. Keep the proportions of the three parts (opening, body, and closing) in mind. For an hour-long presentation, a 5- to 10-minute introduction may be appropriate. For a two-minute farewell gift to a colleague, do not spend one minute explaining why you were chosen to present the memento.

The issue of timing also applies to key points. Time equals importance. Make sure each point gets the time it deserves—no more, no less. Whatever happens, you do not want someone to announce that your time is up when you are only on the second of five points.

A multiplicity of words indicates poverty of thought.

Too many people run out of ideas long before they run out of words.   E. C. MCKENZIE

TIP 88: Prepare Multiple Versions of Various Key Points

When you know that timing may vary, such as when you are one presenter among many on a long agenda, know where you can expand or extract to stay within your allotted time.

If you are preparing a presentation that you may deliver numerous times, consider having a long-, a short-, and a medium-length version of key anecdotes and illustrations. For example, you may plan to use a story about the excellent customer service offered in your organization. You could tell one long anecdote to illustrate the point, a shorter version of that same anecdote, or three very brief anecdotes to make the same point. Or if time is very limited, you may opt to share two key statistics from your customer satisfaction survey and omit the anecdotes altogether.

In other words, have in mind more than one way to make your points—all of them.

TIP 89: Build a Condensed Version of Your Presentation *Before* You're in the Limelight

Assume the worst. Plan what you will cover if your time is unexpectedly cut short: If the client CEO walks into the meeting half an hour late. If a fire alarm goes off before the meeting is to begin, and your presentation slot is reduced by half. If your executive director interrupts to say that he or she has to leave the meeting in five minutes.

If you are using slides for your presentation, you have three choices: (1) Select either an overview slide or a summary slide and use that to make your key points, adding sufficient detail on the most important points. (2) Opt to use your back-up plan—the "custom show." That is, beforehand define a subset of a few key slides that you can use for an abbreviated presentation. Then when you see that your time has been curtailed, select this new, shorter slideshow. (3) Know the slide numbers for a few key slides and go directly to these slides by hitting those numbers, followed by the Enter key.

If you are not using visual support at all, then your job is easier: All you need to do is shuffle your brain to sift out the secondary details and focus on the highlights. This is why you need to know exactly how long it takes to make each point adequately—and to what detail—before you are in the limelight.

OPENINGS THAT ENTICE

TIP 90: Consider Using an "Opening to the Opening"

There are two kinds of openings to a presentation. I call one the *opening to the opening*—comments that refer to the occasion itself. The second opening introduces your topic. Occasionally, the two can be smoothly combined.

The primary purpose of any opening is to get the audience's attention. Television networks spend enormous amounts of money on startling headlines, splashy visuals, engaging teasers and trivia, mood music, and intriguing storyline leaders to keep you tuned in for the upcoming show. Similarly, the introduction you craft for your presentation can either win over or turn off your audience.

Your opening must engage the audience immediately. They will want to listen to you only if they think you can help them, entertain them, or inform them. At the least, they want to know you identify with their feelings, attitudes, or values. Therefore, you have to establish credibility immediately. Why should they listen to you? How are you similar to (or different from) them? What qualifies you to talk on the subject? The opening sets the overall direction of your presentation and lets the audience know what is about to happen and why they should listen.

To arouse interest, to establish rapport and credibility, to give direction—if your opening to the topic does not allow you to accomplish these things, then you may need an opening to the opening.

In an opening to the opening, you can do one or several of the following things:

React to another's introduction of you. "I appreciate your comment on my cycling trip; that should keep me humble during the next 10 minutes." (This lets the audience identify with your embarrassment.)

Disclose something about yourself. "Since Bill brought up college alma maters in his earlier remarks, I'll bet you didn't know that I was pictured on the 'Most Likely to . . .' page of my senior yearbook: 'Most Likely to Have More Clothes than I Could Afford to Send to the Cleaners.' Have you ever been stupid enough to take all your white shirts to the cleaner on the same day? And unlucky enough to have them disappear into a black hole in the back room? Well, guess what? This morning. . . ." (Sharing a personal foible shows vulnerability, allowing the audience to identify with you.)

Comment on the special occasion. "I congratulate you on the silver anniversary of your medical service to the community." (A warm fuzzy will inspire the audience.)

Remember a special date or cause. "On the third anniversary of the traffic accident that claimed so many of our colleagues, I want to go on record as one who remembers their sacrifice." Or "This month marks the second anniversary of the partnership between our companies. We've seen changes in. . . ." (A common, shared experience with the audience evokes positive feelings.)

Compliment the audience. "Many of you have set aside these two days for the meeting at great expense to your own work schedules; you've put caring above your sales commissions." Or "I understand that your organization has won four awards for distinguished achievement in publishing." Or "Thank you for inviting me to join you for your annual golf tournament." (All of these provide warm fuzzies for the audience.)

Respond to the audience's attitude. "I know I'm not addressing an unbiased group on this subject, and I appreciate your willingness to hear my views." Or "I realize that several of you had urgent matters on your schedule when you were asked to attend this presentation, but I can assure you that our issue here is important to your future." (Such comments pique audience members' interest and show your honesty and understanding of their position.)

Refer to something earlier in the program. "As George told his shaggy-dog story earlier, I recalled my similar frustration with such management attitudes." Or "I understand that your staff sessions for the past four months have centered around [the topic]. I want to continue that emphasis, with a slight twist." (These reflections show an interest in the organization and a shared earlier experience.)

Tell about your arrival. "You may think it's easy to drive downtown from the suburbs at 5 A.M. Well, some kind of record must've been set this morning. . . ." (Mentioning that you're susceptible to the same problems others have shows your humanness and often adds humor.)

Reflect on why you were selected for the presentation. "I'm not quite sure why Jennifer asked me to present these ideas when so many of you are equally qualified. Perhaps she just wanted a gen-Xer's view of the issue, without regard for the economics that charge the decision-making atmosphere." (This opening statement piques their curiosity and shows your understanding of the situation.)

Recognize key people in the audience. "Before beginning, I want to thank Vice President Jordan Moore for being here tonight to lend his support to the cause. His active involvement has cleared the necessary channels for organizing this movement throughout the industry in particular. In short, he's put us on the map." (Such comments show admiration and identification with the audience's point of view.)

Express your pleasure at being the presenter. "I want you to know how much I've looked forward to addressing your group tonight. Many of you are old friends who've made me look very good through the years." (Expressing your eagerness to be with them compliments the audience and conveys your sincere gratitude.)

With any opening to the opening, keep your remarks brief—no more than two or three sentences—before moving on to the real introduction to your topic.

TIP 91: Prepare an Opening to the Subject

Do not just "drift into" your subject. Select your opening according to your purpose, the occasion and audience, and your topic. Once you have established rapport, immediately let your audience know that it is to their benefit to hear what you have to say. Keep in mind that your audience is wondering, "What's in it for me? Should I tune out? Sneak out for coffee? Try and catch Geri Savage before she leaves for the day?"

Grab attention; do not just hope for it.

TIP 92: Ask a Rhetorical Question

Examples include "What makes a great leader?" "What would it take to triple our sales in the next two years? Is this wishful thinking or could it be reality?" "Is it possible never to feel depressed again—for any reason?" "Can we improve our health care benefits to employees for less than we're now paying? I'd like to present some figures for your consideration."

TIP 93: Make a Startling Statement

Examples "Your pension funds may not be there when you need them." "One out of four girls between the ages of 10 and 19 will be assaulted sometime during her teens." "One out of three people will need long-term care in a health facility during their lifetime."

TIP 94: Quote an Authority

Examples "The Apostle Paul had confidence in his source of love: 'For I am persuaded that neither death nor life, nor angels nor principalities . . . nor any other created thing, shall be able to separate us from the love of God.' " "Dr. Joseph Stemmons, director of the research project, drew these conclusions from his findings: 'The traces of selenium found in Nevada crude oils are insignificant and will in no way adversely affect the environment.' "

TIP 95: Challenge the Audience

Examples "I dare you to leave tonight unchanged in your attitude about the poverty in our community." "I challenge you to set a quota for your sales territory that will motivate even your best performer." "I urge you to seek out the training you need to acquire the skills that will position you to move ahead in your chosen career." "We need to lay off 12,000 employees in the next 60 days—I need your help to lay out a plan to do it in the least painful way possible."

TIP 96: Declare Your Purpose

Examples: "My purpose is simply to present both sides of this issue." "After you see our designs, I'll request your approval for the funding needed to begin construction immediately." "My hope is that you'll write out a check for any amount—$50, $100, or $1000—to underwrite this memorial." "I plan to introduce you to the project team, tell you a little about each person's responsibilities, and then present our recommendations as a committee."

TIP 97: Brief Your Audience

An example: "I have three points to make tonight. First, our school-age population has increased 48 percent the past 13 months. Second, we don't have adequate school facilities. And third, we're going to have to choose between a tax increase and an inadequate education for our children that will eventually cost us millions of dollars in welfare, crime, and lost wages."

TIP 98: Illustrate an Attitude or Create a Mood

An example: "With the kind of service our support center provides, making a sales call is like walking across a field of firecrackers with a match in your back pocket. Yesterday a customer I'd promised delivery to by August 1 grabbed me by the lapel and threatened a lawsuit. In Atlanta, it's no better."

TIP 99: Reveal a Startling Statistic

Examples: "In the last 3 months, we've spent more than $465,000 on shipping charges." "Our company has increased profits by 380 percent during the last 10 months." "Six to one. That's the new rep-customer ratio."

TIP 100: Mention a Current Event

An example: "This morning's news bombarded us with the plight of the Houston flood victims. Despite this latest disaster, we have yet to convince the majority of our population of the need for appropriate insurance of all kinds—flood, property, life, medical, disability."

TIP 101: Share a Commonality

An example: "How many of you have eaten in a fast-food restaurant at least three times in the last week? [Look around at the raised hands.] Now let me describe the kitchen conditions at the restaurant where I ate breakfast this morning, and *you* tell *me* if we need to push for tighter inspection standards in this city." Another example: "Maybe some of you are having the same difficulties I face in handling these 360-degree performance reviews. Here's what happened to me last week. . . ." Then continue to relate a situation that you think members of the audience can identify with as you make your key point.

TIP 102: Use a Visual Aid

An example: "Look at this necklace against the black velvet. What does its sparkle have to do with mining conditions in Wyoming? I want to point out three things that make this diamond undesirable to our buyers."

TIP 103: Define a Term

An example: "GNC is a term you've seen in the company newsletter for about five issues now. GNC: the Get-Next Command. Think we're talking about computers? No, this term refers to. . . ." Another example: "This year we have one goal: strategic partnerships. Let me define what that means to us—exactly what we're looking for in our supplier relationships."

TIP 104: Compare or Contrast Two Things

Examples: "Men look at garage shelving and say, 'How functional!' Women look at it and say, 'How ugly!' " "Our number-one competitor, Glabbco, has increased its market share by 20 percent during the same period that ours has decreased by 5 percent."

TIP 105: Explain the Significance of Your Topic

An example: "At the conclusion of this study and the related field trips, our dietitians will have gathered enough nutritional information to protect Americans from four dread diseases."

TIP 106: Promise Benefits

General audiences want peace of mind, more money, self-satisfaction, accomplishment, faith, love, approval, and success. Business audiences look for benefits such as increased productivity, lower costs, higher revenue, increased profits, better customer service and satisfaction, less downtime, improved quality, smoother processes, higher retention rates, improved customer loyalty, improved supplier relationships, more profitable strategic partnerships, and more referrals.

The more specific you can be about these issues, the more attention you will garner. For example, "At the conclusion of this presentation, you'll have at your disposal three techniques for increasing your income through your part-time hobby." Or "After this session, you should have a clear, four-step process for solving customer complaints in your department."

TIP 107: Don't Routinely Begin with an Unrelated Joke or Anecdote

Few humorous openings work because the humor rarely has anything to do with the topic and merely leaves the audience hanging. It is like having someone rush up to you in the grocery store with a broad smile and arms extended and then slink away without a word when she realizes she has mistaken you for someone else. Even a funny story that relates to your subject usually works better later in the presentation. At the beginning, the audience is still deciding how to react to you as a person.

TIP 108: Stay Away from the General "Good Morning" or "Good Afternoon"

These greetings almost universally fall flat because they are so common—possibly because they remind us of our school days when we felt obligated to respond, "Good morning, Ms. Jones."

TIP 109: Stay Away from Openings That Focus on "Background," "History," or "Your Story"

The highest point of audience attention is the first few moments. Do not squander those precious minutes with trivia, known information, or boring information. Examples: announcements, the history of the organization or division or product, an organizational chart, and the names and contact information for team members. Another mistake, particularly in sales presentations, is to start with the story of your organization—an "all about us" opening. And all the while, the client wants to know, "But what about *me?* What can you do for *me?*"

Start with the message of interest to the listeners—the "what's in it for them"—not ancient history or ancillary, nice-to-know-sometime information.

TIP 110: Avoid Simply Repeating the Title of Your Talk

If your listeners have read the program and the introducer has mentioned the title in your introduction, your reference will be, at best, anticlimactic. At worst, it will be annoying.

TIP 111: Never Begin with an Apology

Things happen: Planes arrive late, equipment crashes, rooms grow stuffy, and conflicts crowd preparation time. Some or none of these situations may be under your control, and often the audience blames the presenter. But starting with an apology focuses attention on the negative. Generally, it is best to begin with your polished opening to the topic. Then if you feel it necessary to apologize for another situation, do so a little later in a by-the-way comment.

TIP 112: Nix the Negatives

Do not complain about the room setup. Do not denigrate the city or state you are in. Do not explain that you are unprepared. Do not apologize for a boring topic. Do not use offensive language or make prejudicial statements. An opening should arouse interest, establish rapport, and convey credibility to your audience. The following illustrates the difference an appropriate opening can make:

> Uh, I don't know why I'm up here, but I guess it was my unlucky day or something. Anyway, I think I'm supposed to be giving you an update on the Monroe survey. Shipping costs. I've got my notes here somewhere. The gist of our findings is that we're wasting a lot of money at that plant site. And we've got a few suggestions for making some changes throughout the division.

versus

> Would anyone like to take a guess at how much we spent on express shipping services last quarter? Twenty-three thousand dollars in the Monroe office alone! A survey just completed by an independent auditing firm reveals that 85 percent of that cost was waste—shipping charges that could have been avoided with scheduling that met our manufacturing deadlines.

As a result of that study, we have three recommendations for reducing shipping expenditures from $23,000 to less than $3000 over the next 30 days.

Start with credibility so that you can gain attention in order to end with impact.

TIP 113: Promise Only What You Can Deliver

Never tease with benefits that are impossible to attain. If you promise an audience a surefire way to lose 15 pounds in two weeks and then tell them nothing they haven't already tried, they are going to feel disappointed, maybe even angry. If, during a meeting with your boss, you promise to come up with three ways to reduce shipping costs but none turns out to be practical for your office environment, your boss may reasonably assume that you are out of touch with your organization's needs.

SUMMARIES THAT SIZZLE

TIP 114: Deliver Your Formal, Prepared Closing *After* Any Q&A Period

After the body of your presentation, provide a transitional comment, perhaps summarizing your key points to that segment of your presentation, and then pause for the question-and-answer interaction. Then, after the Q&A—whether two minutes or half an hour—deliver your formally prepared, pithy closing comments. Your closing, not the questions, should make the last imprint on the listeners' minds.

TIP 115: Never Apologize in Closing for Not Doing Well or Leaving Out Key Ideas

Only *you* know what you intended to say. Unless you become obviously flustered or comment directly that you have omitted key points, your audience may never know—or care.

TIP 116: Understand the Purpose for Your Summary

"And in closing . . ." makes our ears perk up as listeners, but as a speaker, you want more. You want retention of what you have said. And often you want action.

If your purpose is to inform, your closing may be simply a summary of your key points. If your purpose is to persuade your audience to act—to change an opinion, to make a decision, to approve a purchase, or to support a cause—you will close by calling for a specific next step: enclose a check, give the go-ahead on your project, approve a transfer, fill out an order form, or volunteer to give blood. The action may be immediate or delayed.

If you are presenting to inspire, praise, or motivate, you will want to end with a summary of your commendation or your expectations for the future. You will want to move people to a particular state of mind by touching their emotions. Often you will close this kind of presentation with an emotional anecdote, a fiery quotation, or a prediction for commitment and success.

TIP 117: Signal When You're About to Close

You may begin your closing with a phrase such as, "To wrap up our session . . ."; "One final thought . . ."; "In concluding, I want to relate one last incident about . . ."; "Let me leave you with this idea . . ."; "I'll end with two challenges . . ."; or "To put it succinctly, we must . . ." With these words, your audience members perk up because they are hoping you are going to wrap all they have heard in a nice, neat package.

TIP 118: Summarize Your Key Message

Make sure your audience understands and can summarize in a sentence your key message. If you cannot do it, chances are that they cannot either. This brings you back to the importance of the roadmap as you begin preparation.

TIP 119: Tie the Loop

Think of your speech as a loop; the ending should circle back to the beginning. If you open with a provocative question, be sure to answer it in your closing. If you startle the audience with statistics in your opening, end by telling them how they can change those numbers. If you begin with a hard-luck story, remind them of how the scenario could turn out differently. If you start out with a challenge, leave the audience with the first step in meeting that challenge. If you open with a promise to inform, simply tell them what you told them.

TIP 120: End with a Wallop Rather Than a Whimper

Avoid rumblings and mumblings such as, "I guess that's all I've got to say"; "I think I'm about through unless you have questions"; "That's all they

> We seek to dominate no other nation.
> We ask no territorial expansion. We oppose imperialism.
> We desire reduction in world armaments.
> We believe in democracy;
> we believe in freedom;
> we believe in peace.
> We offer to every nation of the world
> the handclasp of the good neighbor.
> Let those who wish our friendship
> look us in the eye and take our hand.
> — *Franklin D. Roosevelt,*
> *speaking on international affairs*

A strong closing summarizes simply but dramatically.

asked me to say"; "I'm sorry I couldn't get the projector to work, but I hope you got the idea of how the shuttle will look"; "Oh, one thing I forgot to say earlier is that. . . ."

In ending your talk, do not apologize, be long-winded, bring up new points, throw in irrelevant details, change the mood of the group, or shuffle off with no closing at all. Instead, pack a punch. Reinforce your talk with a summary statement, make an appeal, look ahead to the future, ask a rhetorical question, tell an anecdote, quote a well-known authority on the issue, or use a related bit of humor.

Punch the point—do not swallow it.

TIP 121: Never Ramble on Past the Point of High Impact

Anything you say after your polished point of close dilutes your impact. Do not ramble on with anticlimactic drivel. Say it and stop.

THE FINISHING TOUCHES

Anecdotes

TIP 122: Add Anecdotes to Touch All Five Senses

The setting creates the visual. Dialogue engages the ear. And if you can add details that help listeners smell, taste, and feel the atmosphere, you have increased your chances dramatically that they will remember your story and the point it illustrates. If you have ever had music change your mood, then you understand that the senses reach the emotions beyond the intellectual level.

TIP 123: Don't Overlook the Value of Common Experiences as Anecdotal Illustrations

Particularly effective anecdotes are those the group can most identify with—those based on common feelings, predicaments, dilemmas, and decisions that we all experience as humans. Draw from your own experiences, those of "average" people you know, or those of the famous as related in their biographies or TV comments. Read newspapers and magazines with the intention of culling the best stories that might illustrate your topics of interest. Clip them and make a few phone calls or send an e-mail to get the "inside scoop." Often contact information is provided in the story. Those calls or e-mails will provide the extra detail or dialogue to make the story come alive. Also relate the story to family, friends, and coworkers to see what they find intriguing so that you will know what you might highlight in later uses.

Anecdotes make dry points memorable.

TIP 124: Select Several Anecdotes to Illustrate Each Key Point So That You Can Vary Them with Different Audiences

Ideally, one polished anecdote will work with all audiences. In reality, it seldom does. If you speak on one topic often, keep a list of anecdotes from your daily observations and experiences that could illustrate your typical points. Then, when your audiences and occasions vary, you can select the most appropriate.

NOTE: For more tips on anecdotes, see Chapter 8.

Humor

TIP 125: Add Humor Through Anecdotes

The standard line among professional speakers about the importance of humor, even in serious business presentations, goes like this: Question: Do I have to use humor in my presentations? Answer: No—only if you want to get paid. Humor comes through most naturally with anecdotes of personal experiences and observations. For help in embellishing your own stories with humor, see Chapter 8.

TIP 126: Prepare One-Liners to Deliver
"Spontaneously"

> If you do not consider yourself witty on your feet, prepare your one-liners just like the professional comedians do. Select quotations, puns, quips, and colorful phrasing during the preparation phase, and then deliver them as if they are spontaneous.

TIP 127: Add Humor Through Visual Aids

> Examples: a cartoon, a brief video clip, a funny sign that illustrates your issue, photographs of people in odd situations or with humorous expressions.
> Some speakers consider themselves to be their own humorous visual aids. Their contorted body or facial expression gets the laugh.

Quotations

TIP 128: Select Short, Pithy Quotations

> The longer the quotation, the more punch the audience expects it to pack.

TIP 129: Select Quotations from Both the Famous and
the Unknown

> Quotations create impact by adding the words of a recognizable authority. Those which find their way into print are usually succinctly and colorfully worded, crystallizing the key idea better than most presenters could. Here are a few Web sites that put applicable quotations at your fingertips:
>
> *www.quotationspage.com*
>
> *www.quotegeek.com*
>
> *www.bartleby.com*
>
> *www.quoteland.com*
>
> But don't overlook comments by lesser-known individuals and even unknowns. For example, if you are speaking on current problems in the industry, you might interview and share "person on the street" comments gathered from remarks overheard at your trade-show booth at a national convention. These may be anonymous or attributed remarks, depending on which is more important to your point—what they said or who said it.

If you are talking about industry trends, you might extract comments from "Letters to the Editor" in your leading professional journal and present them to your executive strategic planning committee.

If you are talking customer service, comments pulled from recent telephone interviews, from your help desk logs, and from complaint e-mails might be exactly the appropriate illustrations to make your point to your team members.

If speaking to a committee of doctors about the morality of cloning human beings, you may want to find a quotation from a well-respected philosopher, theologian, or scientist.

In short, the notoriety or celebrity status of the author of the remark may or may not be as important to the selection of the quotation as the comment itself.

TIP 130: Let the Quotation Stand on Its Own Merit

You may have heard the macho maxim, "I never complain or explain." If you feel the need to explain the quotation you have selected or to paraphrase it after quoting it, maybe it is not a good selection after all. To explain or paraphrase the quotation dilutes its impact. Use it; pause to give the audience time to consider it, and then move on.

TIP 131: Read a Quotation Directly from Its Source to Add Authority

If you really want to increase credibility for a quotation from a business executive, read it directly from a *Wall Street Journal* or *Fortune* clipping. This is authenticity at its best.

Statistics

TIP 132: Use Statistics with Care

First, make sure they are up to date. Nothing will destroy your credibility like numbers that are five years old. Also, make sure your statistics are not misleading. If your competitor's profit increased by 400 percent last year, that may mean he or she sold four gadgets rather than one. Averages can be deceptive, too. For instance, you wouldn't conclude that a hiker who crossed a desert on a 125-degree afternoon and then plunged into a 41-degree mountain stream experienced an average temperature of 83 degrees during his or her hike.

Be wary of using too many statistics. Bombarding your listeners with numbers confuses them, reducing their chances of recalling any. To make the statistics you select meaningful, frame them in a context your audience can understand. For example, here's a headline from the Scripps Howard News Service: "Taxes cost 163 minutes of every eight working hours." This puts the high cost of taxes in perspective; we work almost 3 hours out of eight to pay them. The writer breaks this figure down further: food and tobacco cost 59 minutes; transportation, 40 minutes; medical care, 39 minutes; clothing, 24 minutes; recreation, 20 minutes; and all other expenses, 50 minutes. Such delineation gives the numbers context and impact.

Remember, it is easier to gather statistics and facts than to make them relevant and memorable. Do not get sidetracked by the first and forget about the second.

TIP 133: Use Both Rounded and Exact Numbers

Exact numbers sound more credible: "The number of single-parent households among our employee population in the Los Angeles office has grown to 83.9 percent" sounds exact and therefore accurate. Rounded numbers, on the other hand, give the appearance of estimations. Yet "slightly less than 85 percent" is easier to remember than "83.9 percent of the employees." So which do you use if you want the numbers to be both credible and memorable? Use the exact number first, and then round it off in later references. Use the exact number in charts; round it off when elaborating on the chart.

TIP 134: Make Statistics Experiential

People digest numbers with great difficulty. Graphs and charts help. But if you can go beyond these common visuals, do so. For example, one manager speaking before his peers at IBM about his budget being cut dramatically yanked off his jacket to reveal his white shirt—with great big holes cut out of the sides and back. Amid the laughter, he made his point dramatically and memorably.

To demonstrate leads turned into closed sales, have your sales group complete a worksheet on "Customer Clyde" who buys X dollars of product Y four times a year. Then increase those leads to customers as the audience calculates on their worksheets. The numbers will come alive as they themselves work with the changing results.

TIP 135: Never Let Facts Speak for Themselves

Facts need interpretation. According to Mark Twain, "There are three kinds of lies: lies, damned lies, and statistics." If you don't believe this, tune into the next political campaign. People can make facts and numbers mean almost anything. Interpret yours so that your listeners draw the same conclusions you intend.

Metaphors, Similes, and Other Analogies

TIP 136: Use Metaphors, Similes, and Other Analogies to Clarify and Aid Retention

A *metaphor* is a word or phrase substituted for another to suggest similarity. For example: "My friend is my Rock of Gibraltar," "Time is money," "Kill that idea," "That question will be the litmus test," "This new line of tires will be our insurance policy against obsolescence."

A *simile* compares two things with the actual words *like* or *as* in the analogy. Recently, I've heard business presenters use examples such as these: "Trying to process these data with your computers is like trying to mow your lawn with a pair of scissors"; "The consistency of this new product is much like shaving foam"; "Your files are like athletic socks and dress socks; you don't need both every day. Access should determine how you should store them"; "This new legislation before Congress is like throwing a nuclear bomb at an ant hill—and missing the ant hill."

The more complex the idea, the more important it is to simplify and illustrate by comparison.

TIP 137: Use Analogies to Provide a Consistent Framework

Think how many times you have heard the functioning of the human eye and its parts compared to the working of a camera—an excellent analogy for clarifying a complex process. Or how often have you heard complex routers referred to as a telephone switchboard—with each part of the equipment explained as it compares to a small telephone system?

Probably the best-known analogies and allegories are Biblical parables and Aesop's fables. "Concern over the unrepentant means leaving the 99 sheep to look for the lost one." "The tortoise runs a slow but steady pace and crosses the finish line a winner." Such visual or emotional analogies help audiences follow a lengthy presentation step by step.

TIP 138: Remember That Analogies Never Prove Anything

They illustrate. They clarify. They make points memorable. When you stretch them for proof, they fail.

Colorful Phrasing

TIP 139: Use Triads to Tease the Ear

Triads refer to words, phrases, or sentences grouped in threes. Examples: "Blood, sweat, and tears"; "Faith, hope, and charity"; "Ready, set, go"; "Government of the people, by the people, for the people"; "Our service is quick, safe, and reliable"; and "It's a turnkey option: delivered, installed, and trained."

TIP 140: Use Alliteration to Play and Pay

Alliteration refers to words that start with the same sound or rhyme in other ways. Such alliteration can help your audience remember your key points or your positioning statements. Examples: "Prepare, promote, and produce." "They're playing the blame game." "Our contracts are clean, clear, concise." "Assess your needs, access your database, allocate your resources, and apply our technology."

TIP 141: Use Antithesis to Reverse Thinking

Opposite ideas juxtaposed in the same sentence create thought-provoking grabbers: Examples: "Ask not what your country can do for you; ask what you can do for your country." "The real question is not, Can you afford this equipment; the real question is, Can you afford the downtime without it?" "The problem isn't the problem; the problem is the supposed solution."

TIP 142: Select Slogans to Encapsulate Your Theme

Slogans typically capture a key point in a memorable way. Salespeople have created their own slogans, such as "Dialing for dollars" or "Satisfaction guaranteed or your money back," as have most organizations, associations, and corporations.

As you repeat your slogan throughout the presentation—or at least at the beginning and the end—you add emphasis to the key message. Here are examples from our social or political history that remain in our collective memory primarily because they were captured in a slogan that resounded on the airwaves for days or decades: "The race card"; "Just say no"; "Compassionate conservatism"; "Read my lips"; and "An axis of evil."

TIP 143: Repeat for Purpose and Effect

Readers can always flip back the page and reread if they miss a point. Listeners cannot. So a functional reason for planned repetition is to make sure your audience is "with you"—that they haven't missed a point somewhere along the way.

Another reason to repeat a key word or phrase is simply for effect. Motivational speakers use repetition almost as frequently as a pause—to let an idea sink in and soak in.

TIP 144: Create Mnemonic Aids

After you have organized your five steps to do X or your six goals for the new year, consider ways to help your audience members recall them quickly. Can you create an acrostic? (An *acrostic* is built by using the first letter of each idea to form a single word or phrase or sentence.) The acrostic holds the concept together so that it is easy to remember as a whole. Here's an example:

Acrostic = A Fun Day!

A = ample money

F = friends

U = unscheduled time

N = no interruptions

D = date

A = adventures

Y = youthful energy

Or rather than an acrostic, you may collapse a complex formula or plan into four short words that will be easier to remember. Sometimes the mnemonic might be visual—for example, a drawing of a three-legged stool with each leg labeled with a different product line that produces total revenue for the division.

However you determine to do it, such devices greatly improve retention of your concepts.

Transitions

TIP 145: Polish Your Transitions Between Points

Once you have decided on the framework for your key points, be sure to tie them together. Transitions carry your listener from point A to point B. Each point should conclude with a bridging statement that leads the audience to the next key point, as shown in the following examples:

Example 1

Concluding point A: "Good health depends not only on stress reduction but also on proper nutrition."

Bridge: "So you can see how eating right reduces the risks of heart disease and cancer."

Overview of point B: "Let's talk about what we mean by proper nutrition in our company cafeteria."

Example 2

Bridge: "You may be thinking that all those preventive measures sound good. But where will you find the time to implement them?"

Overview: "We've decided on three ways to help you stay healthy without lengthening your work day. The first is our intent to install a jogging track."

Concluding point and bridging to next: "So the jogging track should be open by the end of the year. In the meantime, of perhaps even greater concern is the dietitian's meal plan. . . ."

In addition to these transitional passages, there are several other ways to signal your audience that you are ready to move to the next idea. These include a summary of your points up to this juncture in your presentation, a long pause, a change of physical location in the room, or a new visual. Whichever method you use, take your listeners with you as you move from thought to thought.

Smooth transitions increase retention and exemplify a polished presentation. Transitions are to a speech what paragraphs are to a document.

TIP 146: Limit Your Use of the Common Countdown

The most common transitional device is to enumerate: "My first reason for wanting to change the current policy is. . . . The second reason we should consider a change is. . . . The third reason for the change involves. . . . And finally, we need a change because. . . ." There's nothing wrong with this approach other than it is just not very imaginative.

TIP 147: Use a Series of Questions as Transitions

Your entire presentation may be arranged around a framework of questions as transitions. For example: What's the problem? How serious is the problem? How do we solve the problem? Who should be assigned to tackle the problem? How long will it take? How much will it cost?

TIP 148: Consider a Theme Transition

Look for a theme or metaphor to use as a transitional hinge between presentation segments. For example, consider this one built around the theme of myths: "The first competitor myth that I'd like to dispel among our sales team is that. . . . Another myth that we need to allay is. . . . Another pervasive myth in the marketplace is that. . . ."

A second example: "Our department has been holding onto security blankets far too long to generate revenue. One security blanket for last year was our income from product *X*. . . . Another security blanket that we came to depend on in the third quarter was. . . . Then there was the security blanket of revenue from product *Y* that we grabbed and clung to in the fourth quarter. . . ."

In addition to providing excellent transitions, these metaphors create memorable images in listeners' minds.

Titles

TIP 149: Eliminate the Deadwood: The Obvious, the Unnecessary, and the General

Because you need so many precise, descriptive words for technical and business presentations, you have absolutely no room for the deadwood. Eliminate "garbage" words and phrases such as these: a history of . . . , the use of . . . , a study of . . . , a report on . . . , an investigation into . . . , various aspects of . . . , several approaches to . . . , various techniques to . . . , an analysis of the performance of . . . , and factors in. . . .

TIP 150: Use the Primary Title to Grab Attention and a Subtitle to Explain

The primary title can be intriguing or straightforward, humorous or serious. In general, avoid long titles that obscure or mislead as to subject or tone. Use a subtitle to give the real skinny. Here are some ideas for creating a catchy title. Focus on a specific. Be global and comprehensive.

Sound useful, not cute. Sound cute, not serious. Try alliteration and rhyming. Pose contrasting ideas. State benefits. Combine several of the foregoing.

Once you are holding a stack of notes or a full outline and draft of your presentation, you will feel much better about the business of presenting a new budget to your boss or a new product line to your prospect. Getting your message down in black and white is reassuring and motivating. However, you are not ready to deliver your ideas yet. Editing comes next.

THE EDIT

If you do not edit yourself *before* speaking, your listeners will do it *as* you speak. If you seem hurried or behind schedule and in danger of not finishing on time, the members of your audience will keep one eye on their watches and the other on your stack of notes or the number of your visuals. *Their* anxiety will become *your* anxiety.

To put your audience at ease, assure them that you are in control of your information by pacing yourself and staying on schedule. Practice gives you confident control. Despite your attention to timing from the very start of your preparation, you will need to edit during your practice sessions as a final measure.

TIP 151: Weed Out Generalities, Clichés, and Platitudes

Forget what you learned in school—more is not better. No one grades by pages, weight, or length anymore. Make your points specific, and support them with facts. Substitute fresh wording for clichés. Do not put your audience to sleep with platitudes.

If you don't edit yourself *before* you speak, your listeners will do it *as* you speak.

TIP 152: Remember That Timing Indicates Emphasis

In general, a good rule of thumb for allocation of your overall time is to spend 10 to 15 percent of your time on the opening, 70 to 85 percent on the body, and 5 to 10 percent on the closing. This allows slightly more time up front in the introduction to grab attention, "win over" a hostile or uninterested audience, and establish credibility than to close the presentation. If your presentation includes an involved action plan, that section most likely should be part of the body of your presentation, and your close should focus on the final persuasive push toward the decision to act.

If, during practice, you find that you spend 30 seconds defending a reason to spend $10,000 and seven minutes on an introductory anecdote, that is the time to reshuffle your information so that the timing of these two segments more accurately reflects the importance of the ideas.

To lengthen the entire presentation, come up with additional key points or elaboration for emphasis: facts, statistics, illustrations, quotations, surveys, or anecdotes. Do not simply add words to points already well made.

On the other hand, you may discover that you need to cut. In doing so, always keep the audience's preferences in mind. Think of your presentation as a roadmap. If your audience wants to take only interstate highways to their destination, do not pencil in all the farm-to-market roads along the way. This merely clutters the map.

The secret of being a bore is to tell everything.
VOLTAIRE

On information overload: Remember, most houseplants in the U.S. are killed by overwatering.   R. JOHN BROCKMANN

TIP 153: Record Your Timing Point by Point

Plan how long you intend to spend on each point of your presentation. Then later, as you rehearse your presentation, make any necessary adjustments to that plan and record the time required to deliver each section. For example, if a certain anecdote takes three minutes, jot this on your outline. These notations will help you make spur-of-the-moment decisions about what to eliminate or add if you run long or short during the actual presentation. Here's an example:

3. Explanation about delay in relocation overseas—5 min

   Statistics from Atlanta office—2 min

   Jamie Huang's move—2 min

   Second-quarter foul-ups—1 min

Notice that the total point takes five minutes. However, if the client team arrives at the meeting a few minutes late, the presenter may decide to recoup two minutes of lost time by omitting the Jamie Huang anecdote from this point and another five minutes from another place in the presentation.

TIP 154: Deliver and Time Your Presentation in Several Run-Throughs

If you are reading a script or practicing with an outline, remember that one page (about 250 words) translates to about two minutes of spoken delivery. To be accurate, read and clock your presentation several times. Keep in mind a speaker's tendency to present a talk more quickly in rehearsal than in real life.

No matter how closely you have timed your presentation, however, it is rarely a good idea to set your slideshow to run automatically. It makes an otherwise great presentation look far too canned and therefore imperfect. Leave timed, automatically running slideshows for unnarrated presentations at a trade show or the museum lobby!

TIP 155: Cut the Fat First

Sometimes you can condense your presentation without deleting anything of substance simply by tightening your wording. If you have written a draft, strip away the fat. Note how succinct the quotations are at the beginning of each chapter in this book. They convey their ideas with nouns and verbs. Adjectives and adverbs clutter. For stronger impact, retain only the meat of the idea.

TIP 156: Cut the Skeleton, Not the Flesh, If You Must Reduce Length

If your presentation runs too long, you may be tempted to cut the flesh and leave the skeleton. That is, you may feel inclined to retain all your key points and just omit some of the elaboration about each—the statistics, stories, quotations, and visuals. Don't. Remember, these "extras" make your key points memorable. It is better to make fewer points well than to make many points that no one remembers.

TIP 157: Always Leave Yourself a Safety Net on Timing

Count on the fact that a written presentation will take longer to deliver with ad libs, audience reactions, and interactivity. Distractions, late starts, questions, and other interruptions may force you to do some on-the-spot adjustments to end on time.

5

Practicing Your Presentation

By failing to prepare you are preparing to fail.
BEN FRANKLIN

There are three things to aim at in public speaking: first to get into your subject, then to get your subject into yourself, and lastly to get your subject into your heart. A. S. GREGG

Oratory: The art of making deep sounds from the chest seem like important messages from the brain. FRANKLIN P. JONES

How necessary is rehearsal? The best of his day, Mark Twain had this to say: "It usually takes more than three weeks to prepare a good impromptu speech."

Reading from a full script, speaking from notes or an outline, and memorizing your speech—these are your delivery choices until technology makes it possible and affordable for each of us to have a portable teleprompter the size of a PDA.

Speaking from notes or an outline is by far the superior method. On occasion, however, the other two options have merit. In complex presentations containing technical data difficult to learn, memorize, or summarize, you may resort to reading a prepared text for portions of the presentation. On other occasions, such as formal situations with legal implications, a formal statement that must be delivered precisely may be read.

TIP 158: Consider the Pros and Cons Before Reading a Script

Nothing can lull an audience to sleep faster than hearing a speaker read a speech.

Pros

- A script quiets your fears that you will "go blank." Having every word in front of you in black and white provides a security blanket.

- Your timing will be perfect. You will know exactly how long each point takes, and with practice in reading, you will feel confident about ending on time.

- Your language will be more exact, precise, colorful, and grammatically correct than if you speak extemporaneously. You will have the opportunity to rework and polish each sentence.

- You generally can include a greater amount of detail with fewer words by reading a tightly edited script.

- You can create and maintain a formal atmosphere for the presentation.

- You will have something "official" to give to the media if you are a spokesperson for your organization. Scripts are often necessary for gaining approval of your wording from your company's public affairs officer or if you are otherwise concerned about being misquoted. You can, however, provide a written text to the media for their quotes and still deliver your talk extemporaneously.

Cons

- You will have little eye contact with your audience. No matter how much you have practiced your upward glances, you will be tempted to read more and more—particularly in the all-important beginning, when you either win or lose your audience's attention. The reciprocity of the situation is lost. When you speak to an audience eye to eye, you have their attention because they have yours. When you stare at the script, their temptation is to reciprocate by looking at their own notes or glancing around the room at others' reactions.

- Your words lose their genuineness and intimacy. When you cannot look your audience in the face, you lose one of your strongest sources of credibility. Imagine if Don Juan, in wooing a foreign sweetheart, pulled a scrap of paper from his pocket and read in her language, "I love you for your beauty, your warmth, your charm, your thoughtfulness." How romantic can this moment be when she's gazing at his eyes and he's staring at a piece of paper?

- You will not sound natural. Despite your skill as an experienced lecturer, you will have difficulty not sounding stilted when reading from a script—much like the "average Joe" testimonials on TV commercials.

- Your gestures will be nonexistent or contrived. To be effective, gestures should come from the gut. Reading stifles that unconscious signal to gesture where necessary.

- You will be tied to a lectern or table to deliver your presentation, forfeiting the freedom to move toward your visuals or the audience.

- You may lose your place. If panic sets in, you may find yourself frantically groping for your next phrase or idea.

- The audience may wonder if the words and ideas you are delivering are really yours—or if a ghostwriter friend or colleague drafted them. And, if so, should you receive credit for the presentation's impact?

- If it is an audience you know well, they will contrast the way you usually talk and gesture with your "presentation style" and focus on the disparity between the two.

As you will discover, the advantages of reading from a script can be achieved with almost any delivery method if you prepare adequately. The cons are hard to overcome. Only on rare occasion should you read from a script.

READING FROM A SCRIPT

If, against all advice from the experts, you decide to read your presentation, here are some tips to make you more effective.

TIP 159: Dictate the Text in One Sitting

The process will be faster, and the tone will be more informal and appropriate. After you have a draft, you can polish it.

TIP 160: Prepare Your Script for Reading by Marking It

Double- or triple-space the text. Leave extra lines between paragraphs to signal yourself that you are finished with an idea. Type using both upper- and lowercase letters; all uppercase words are more difficult to read.

Mark a single slash (/) to indicate a pause; mark a double slash (//) to indicate a longer pause. With a highlighting pen, mark key words and phrases that need emphasis. Choose certain colors to help you quickly grasp the layout of your ideas. For example, use green for basic key points, yellow for examples, red for statistics, and blue for transitions and recaps.

Leave the pages unstapled so that you can lay them aside easily as you finish reading each one. Do not break a sentence, paragraph, or list between two pages. Always number the pages. Insert margin notes for use of visuals, demonstrations, or other movements away from the lectern—all in the wide right-hand margins.

Always deliver your speech from the same copy you used for practice rather than a new copy with a different layout. Your mind will "photograph" chunks of text, and the first words of a paragraph will help your brain recall the rest.

TIP 161: Check the Lighting at the Lectern or Table Beforehand

Nothing perplexes a speaker like getting to the lectern to read a perfectly marked script only to discover that the lighting is so bad that either the main text appears only faintly or any colored highlighting fails too show up at all.

TIP 162: Don't Try to Hide Your Script

The audience will know that you are reading, so trying to hide the script will look deceptive and silly.

TIP 163: Slow Down

Be aware that you probably will read too quickly and will need to make a conscious effort to slow down. Make yourself notes on your script to do so.

TIP 164: Concentrate on the Meaning Rather Than the Phrasing of Your Words

Read with understanding. With concentration, your inflection, pauses, and gestures will improve.

SPEAKING FROM NOTES OR AN OUTLINE

TIP 165: Speak from Notes or an Outline When
Delivering Most Presentations

Although there are exceptions, this is by far the most effective delivery method for the majority of presenters. For the sake of argument, however, here are the pros and cons for your own evaluation:

Pros

- You can maintain the all-important eye contact with the audience throughout.
- Your ideas will seem genuine and intimate because they will be expressed spontaneously, with your natural inflection and emotion.
- Your gestures will be natural.
- Notes provide both an outline for security and the freedom to use visuals or to interact with the audience.
- You will have no fear about adding or deleting ideas, facts, or illustrations to suit audience needs or reactions. Also absent is the fear of losing your place and your poise and of trying to find the right spot in the script to jump back in.

Cons

- Your exact phrasing will not be as precise with an outline as with a polished script.
- Your timing will vary.

High-impact content does not happen seat-of-the-pants. In addition to the idea wheel technique used for generating ideas and organizing them into the general speech framework, you probably will need two more outlines for most presentations longer than about 30 minutes: a practice outline and a delivery outline. The content flows in direct proportion to the time you spend organizing your ideas and then polishing them for a *smooth* delivery.

TIP 166: Practice with a "Half and Half" Outline

A practice outline is a detailed outline on multiple pages or cards. If you are using slides, the Notes View of your presentation software package allows you to put your outline directly beneath corresponding slides. However, I

> *5 min.*
>
> **Transition:** "So, how can we dig our way out of the paperwork blizzard?"
>
> **3. Give your people a challenge.**
> • Survey responses—28% "unchallenged"
> • Anecdote—utility company
> • Statistics from Garfield
>
> **Conclusion:** "Clearly, our people should be able to volunteer for advisory committees."

The half-and-half script provides structure and security while allowing flexibility and fresh phrasing. Use it for practice or delivery.

do not suggest starting your outline there because the tendency will be to build your entire presentation around your slideshow—a bad habit! The slideshow then becomes your presentation. It is far better to start with an outline of key points elsewhere and then cut and paste those portions that relate to a specific slide into your presentation software.

The benefit of such detail is a memory crutch for practice. The negatives are that you are likely to fumble with the pages during delivery and refer to the outline too frequently, losing eye contact with your audience and destroying credibility. The half-and-half script combines features of a full script (opening, transition, and conclusion) with key words as memory joggers for main points. See the figure above for specifics.

With this method, you write opening statements, transitions, and conclusions in polished form. Then you express the "meat" of each point using key words only. Such ideas will receive a spontaneous and fresh delivery in the final presentation.

TIP 167: Deliver Your Presentation with a Key-Word Outline

For your actual delivery, construct an outline containing only key words that will trigger your memory with just a glance.

TIP 168: Create a System to Manage Your Notes, Outline, or Slides Effectively During Delivery

No audience will mind that you use notes. After all, they want to know that you are prepared. The issue is *how* you use them. Here are a few guidelines to help you handle your notes, outline, or slides effectively during delivery:

- Always number items, but feel free to reshuffle them as needs change.

- Jot down how much time each point or illustration takes so that you can make an on-the-spot decision about what to eliminate or add if time runs short or long.

- Color-code the edges of your cards, pages, or slides so that you can quickly skip forward or backward if you make extemporaneous changes. For example, use green edges or highlight colors for main points, blue for supporting points or illustrations, and red for statistics. (More about this in the Visuals chapter.)

TIP 169: Memorize the Opening, Transitions, and Closing

The first and last few minutes have the highest impact. Memorizing your opening, transitions, and close allows you to look at your audience and deliver your points with conviction and freshness.

TIP 170: Practice with Any Visuals or Demonstrations that You Plan to Use in Actual Delivery

A mental walk-through will not do, even if you plan to use notes. You need to practice the timing. Additionally, actual practice with demonstrations or visuals often will reveal "gaps" either in your content or in your visuals—places they do not match, items out of order, builds that should appear all at once, or other confusing animation.

MEMORIZING YOUR SPEECH

The final presentation method is memorization. My suggestion is *not* to memorize anything longer than 10 minutes. You will fear going blank, particularly if there are distractions. Memorization also makes the audience uneasy. At first, they marvel, then they worry whether you will make it to the end. Here are the pros and cons, along with a few tips in case you decide on this delivery option.

Pros

- If you work very hard to memorize a long script verbatim, with all the appropriate inflections and gestures, you will sound like a genius—although maybe a robot genius.
- It will take you a long time—a very long time.

Cons

- If you have a memory lapse, you will feel like an idiot, and your audience will think you foolish for being so "unprepared."

TIP 171: Prepare a Written Text and Read It and Reread It and Reread It

Practice from the same script, because your mind's eye will "photograph" sections of pages to aid memorization. Repetition is your secret weapon.

TIP 172: Break Your Script into Chunks

Memorize one chunk at a time. Then, as you practice, recite the previously memorized chunks each day, and add on the newly learned one.

TIP 173: Devise an Acronym or Other Mnemonic Device to Help with Recall

Some people plan their shopping list this way; others, their to-do list. The use of acronyms or visual pictures (such as associating each floor of your executive suite with a concept or comparing a Halloween costume to parts of the marketing campaign) will keep you from going blank.

TIP 174: Practice in Front of a Mirror

You will be more likely to verify that you are retaining natural facial expressions and other appropriate gestures.

LEARNING—BUT NOT MEMORIZING OR READING—YOUR MATERIAL

TIP 175: Read Your Outline, Notes, or Practice Script Over and Over

Read aloud to time yourself on each section, and record the times in the margins. Connect the ideas using an acronym, and try to predict the next thought before your eyes catch the next prompt. Then practice in front of a mirror to see how often you are able to glance up from your notes.

TIP 176: Memorize the Opening, Transitions, and Closing

Memorization at these points will allow you to maintain eye contact at the most important times—when you are making a first impression (and your audience is deciding whether you are worth listening to) and at the conclusion (when they fix in their minds how good you were).

TIP 177: Scrimmage—There's No Substitute

A mental "walk through" alone will not do. Practice expressing your key ideas aloud, in complete sentences, and in the correct order. The time you spend on these drills will add polish and confidence to your actual presentation. Pay particular attention to your delivery of humorous anecdotes. They, more than any other part of your presentation, tend to succeed or fail based on delivery.

Videotape yourself to become aware of your posture, gestures, and facial expressions. Either turn your back to the monitor as you listen to your recording or make an audio recording to study your voice. You will become more aware of your rate of speech, a tendency to let words trail off at the ends of sentences, mumbling, or poor diction. This aids you in deciding where to add emphasis and variety.

Another benefit of audiotape is that you can listen to and fix the material in your mind while completing other tasks, such as commuting to work, exercising, or eating. Tape. Listen. Rehearse again. Tape. Listen. Rehearse, and record again. You will hear dramatic improvements with each trial run, and these improvements will build your confidence.

Finally, practice in front of friends, family, or colleagues, and solicit their feedback. If they are interested, your enthusiasm and confidence will grow. If their attention wanders, you need either more practice or better material.

Sure, scrimmaging seems like a waste of time on the front end. But the payoff is tremendous. Scrimmaging reveals gaps in your content in time for you to repair them. It helps you coordinate the visual support so that things flow more smoothly and you can concentrate on your transitions between points. It helps you polish your phrasing into catchy, attention-getting statements. And it builds your self-confidence. All these factors then affect energy, passion, and ultimately, your credibility with the audience.

TIP 178: Evaluate and Incorporate Feedback from the Practice Sessions

Remember that others' feedback will be biased. Your family and friends generally will praise your presentation. Do not rely too heavily on their compliments; instead, focus on their suggestions. Conversely, do not take too seriously the harsh comments of a perpetual critic.

- Value your self-confidence over comments that are more destructive than constructive.

- Do not try to correct everything at once. Have a priority system. Work on either slowing down your delivery, adding gestures, or remembering your transitions. One thing at a time.

- Keep an eye peeled for flawed logic or information gaps that need closing—even at this late date. The practice phase is your last chance to ensure that ideas are logical and clear.

- Continue to monitor your timing, and remember that your actual delivery will tend to run a little longer than your practice.

- Do not be too hard on yourself. Remember that you will always sound better to others than to yourself. Focus on your improvements and how much your audience will benefit from listening to you.

With a little editing, a little learning, a little practice, and a little evaluation, your material will become so much a part of you that the ideas will flow when you open your mouth.

6

Presenting Technical Information to Nontechnical Audiences

That must be wonderful; I don't understand it at all.   MOLIERE

When I can't talk sense, I talk metaphor.
                                        J. P. CURRAN

I might not know how to use 34 words where three would do, but that doesn't mean I don't know what I'm talking about.   RUTH SHAYS

Do not accustom yourself to use big words for little matters.   SAMUEL JOHNSON

Broadly speaking, the short words are the best, and the old words best of all.
                                        SIR WINSTON CHURCHILL

Think like a wise man but communicate in the language of the people.
                                        WILLIAM BUTLER YEATS

Humorist Will Rogers once observed, "We're all ignorant—only on different subjects." Translating technical concepts to laypersons rather than other technical colleagues requires a different mindset, more attention to detail, and a higher skill set.

Scratching below the surface, you understand why this is the case: (1) You cannot just dump the details and expect laypeople to make sense of it all—to sort the trivial from the significant, make assumptions, and come to the same conclusions as you do. (2) You have to think of creative ways to explain complex concepts that avoid references to background, jargon, or short-cut thinking in the same amount of time as you would ordinarily use. (3) You typically have to adopt an entirely new viewpoint on the information and data—to apply it to other purposes.

TIP 179: Keep Asking Yourself "So What?"

Technical presenters used to speaking to other technical professionals often assume that the information they share points the audience to clear conclusions. It does not.

Facts rarely speak for themselves. They need interpretation. To keep yourself on target with a nontechnical group, continually ask yourself "So what?" as you prepare. Then, do not forget to add the "So what this means to you/us/the organization/the bottom line is that . . ." to every point.

And when you come to a section of details where you cannot look the group squarely in the eye and complete the statement "So what this means to you is . . . ," this is generally a clear indication that you should omit these details.

TIP 180: Never Decide That Your Content Dwarfs Your Delivery

The philosophical nature of many technical professionals demands that they be thorough and precise. This is why such professionals often go overboard in creating visuals—too many, too cluttered, and too meaningless. The visuals serve as notes so that they can remember every single detail, and what they do not remember to say, the audience members can read for themselves.

Being thorough in your preparation is always a good idea, but when you start to prepare slides, err on the side of fewer rather than more. Yes, your content typically generates your invitation to speak. That said, your delivery can be so dull and painful that your audience simply cannot absorb your content. Both delivery and content count.

TIP 181: Know When to Be Persuasive, Not Just Informative

One of the biggest hurdles technical presenters face is changing their mindset about their mission. When our instructors conduct oral presentation workshops for technical groups and come to the section on shaping their content, someone invariably pushes back with this comment: "But we're not supposed to draw conclusions and make recommendations. They [usually meaning the senior executives] just want the technical perspective as a basis for drawing their own conclusions."

Seldom is this the case. Technical presenters are valuable to their audiences precisely because they guide the group to draw the appropriate conclusions based on the technical data.

In short, take a viewpoint about your data.

TIP 182: Avoid a Data Dump

Think of your data or technical information as a lump of clay. To make it useful, you have to shape it. For the most part, each audience will prefer a different shape. Some will prefer an indoor flowerpot. Some will prefer a large patio planter. Some will prefer a brick retaining wall on which to display the flowerpot.

Therefore, you may have to build a new mold for each reiteration of your presentation. And even if you can use the same general mold (structure) for multiple groups, you will need to select your details carefully and then regroup and reorder them in the way that makes most sense to match the interest and needs of your specific audience.

If you find yourself presenting on any given project, using the same set of slides, making the same key points, and elaborating with the same details, you probably are off target and in danger.

TIP 183: Prefer the "Us" Versus "You" Tone

In our culture, we tend to hold the person with the most information at a higher status. And that higher status can erect a barrier with an audience. Expert, teacher, critic, peer, guide, or motivator—each is appropriate in certain situations. The trick is deciding which to use with any given audience. In general, adopt an "us" tone rather than a didactic one. In a contest between "eloquent but cold" and "adequate but cordial," the latter tends to make a stronger impact and pry open more minds.

TIP 184: Use the Precise, Technical Word—But Only When You Need It

In shopping for jewelry, you know that the most ornate, gaudy settings do not necessarily mean the highest quality gold. The same is true for showy language that calls attention to itself rather than to the idea it conveys. Why refer to weeds around the warehouse as "vegetation around the exterior periphery of the storage facility"?

Use the precise word without being unduly technical. There is a difference. Mark Twain observed, "The difference between the right word and the almost right word is the difference between lightning and the lightning bug." As a technical professional, you certainly do not want to misuse words that you will need for accuracy on technical topics. However, neither do you want to use technical jargon when a nontechnical word conveys the idea just as well.

TIP 185: Limit Your Visuals to the Necessary Few

It is understandable why technical presenters tend to use so many visuals: Their information is, well, technical and therefore tedious to commit to memory. Therefore, the charts become their notes. However, put yourself in the chairs of your typical audience—for four hours, eight presenters, and 293 slides. This is death by mouse click! With every slide you are tempted to display, ask: "Is this absolutely necessary to my bottom-line message?"

If in doubt, leave it out. (If your fingers itch to create the data slide as your notes, have at it—then hide it! Or provide the data as a handout or in a report.)

NOTE: For tips on slide design and use, see Chapter 9.

7
Persuasion— Everybody's in Sales

If you can't convince them, confuse them.
HARRY S. TRUMAN

Use soft words and hard arguments.
ENGLISH PROVERB

If you truly mean to persuade a man, you must have his goodwill. Your approach must be disarming so that he does not assume an attitude of defense. You must not seem to be opposing your conviction to his, challenging him to a contest in which his pride is at stake. On the contrary, you must be friendly and show respect for the quality of his mind, avoiding any implication of superiority on your part. To show off your own wit is merely to discredit your wisdom.
LOUIS J. HALLE, JR.

What orators lack in depth, they make up for in length.
BARON DE MONTESQUIEU

Many people consider persuasive presentations to a client or boss the most difficult of all because there is so much at stake in the audience's action or inaction—a commission check, a promotion, a career.

Yet practice in persuasion has been plentiful: Have you ever persuaded a professor to change a grade? A store clerk to give you a refund—against published policy? A traffic cop to let you off with only a warning ticket? A seller to negotiate a discount? A date to go out with you? Someone to marry you? A teenager to stay in school? A bureaucrat to make an exception?

Everybody is in sales. Your job may be to sell your ideas, conclusions, budget, plans, products, or services to an audience of 2, 20, or 2000.

TIP 186: Determine Your Persuasive Structure Based on Biases

Strategy 1 (Use with Neutral Audiences)

State the message up front—your key conclusions and exactly what decision or action you want from the audience. Presenters often fall into the trap of trying to "lay the groundwork" before getting to the key action or attitude they want from listeners. They fear that stating a key recommendation or desired action up front is, well, too "up front."

In the business setting, however, decision makers become restless with the delayed approach. They wonder what you are leading up to and why you are being so cagey. Even in other settings, the roundabout approach makes audiences squirm. They want the to-the-point, journalistic storyline before deciding to stay tuned. In fact, buyers frequently interrupt sellers in the middle of a lengthy pitch with, "Excuse me, but what exactly are you selling?" So cut to the chase. Don't keep your audience guessing about your intentions.

Strategy 2 (Use When the Audience Has a Slight Bias Against Your Conclusions and Recommended Action)

Decide whether you want to diplomatically refute other solutions or points of view or merely support your own. You may unnecessarily anger audience members who adhere to the opposing viewpoint if you continually focus on the fallacy of their thinking. You may have more success simply by building your case and letting them come to realize the ripples in their own reasoning.

Strategy 3 (Use When the Audience Has a Strong Bias Against Your Conclusions and Recommended Action)

If you know that your listeners will be dead set against what you propose, begin by discussing the drawbacks of all other alternatives, and then follow with your own proposal. Present your supporting arguments in most-to-least-important arrangement.

If you do not attempt to control the reasoning of your audience by your structure, your listeners may agree with each fact you present and still arrive at a totally different conclusion.

TIP 187: Use the Principle of Scarcity

With a gas station on every corner, you do not worry much about a low fuel tank. If the price of gasoline posted on one service station sign looks too high, you drive on down the road to compare prices. But your behavior changes dramatically when you are about to enter the desert with a less-than-full tank and see a sign that reads: "Last gasoline station for the next 180 miles."

You can use this same principle of scarcity when you are selling ideas. Point out limitations—ideas, time frame, budget, workers—and see if you do not increase the impact of your words and speed up decisions.

TIP 188: Use the Principle of Reciprocity

Three parties—a neighbor, the City of Grapevine, and I—all went together to buy a strip of raw land as investment property along an interstate about 15 years ago. The then-owner refused to subdivide the acreage in smaller lots, and it took all three of us to pool our resources to make the purchase.

The only remaining issue was the overgrowth of trees and grass on the land. However, every time we would get a call from the city that the acreage needed to be mowed, our neighbor who had bought the adjoining land offered to take care of it for us when he took care of his parcel of land.

I appreciated it and offered to pay my half of the bill. However, he refused to let me reimburse him.

Result: Every time a restaurant chain, hotel, or bank has approached him wanting to buy his corner lot but needing additional acreage, he has asked us about our willingness to sell our property with his. Even though we have had plans all along to use the land for our own building, guess our answer? This is the *principle of reciprocity*. Somebody does something nice for you—no matter how big or small—and you feel compelled to return the favor.

When presenting, you can use this same principle by "giving" your audience something: paying a sincere compliment, acknowledging that their viewpoint or situation has validity, agreeing with them about the difficulty of their decision or job, ensuring their physical comfort, or paying them respect. When it comes time to accept your ideas, they often feel obligated to go along.

TIP 189: Determine Whether to Use a Positive or a Negative Appeal

Consider "You'll live longer and feel better if you exercise" versus "If you don't exercise, your chances of getting heart disease are increased by 42 percent." Both appeals work—but not always with the same type of audience. A difficult goal as a presenter is to identify which appeal works best with which group.

TIP 190: Use a One-Track Approach

Avoid hedging, wishy-washy statements: "I'm not completely up to date on this, but . . ."; "Well, I know there are two sides to this issue, and you probably can find some holes in my argument, but . . ."; "I understand where the marketing people are coming from, and they have a point. But my point is . . ." "We probably could make this thing work either way, depending on how you want to look at the numbers. There are always two sides to any issue."

Most likely your audience already knows all sides and points of the issue. Generally, the best strategy is to focus on yours—factually and with adequate preparation.

TIP 191: Identify and Use Meaningful Proof

Many presenters have wasted enormous amounts of time gathering proof of their points—only to discover that their audience did not agree that the studies, surveys, focus-group findings, or work samples proved anything.

Make the proof meaningful to those whose opinions count. For example, you may prove that the new engine from vendor A is faster than any on the market and will solve all your backlogged welding projects. However, if your executive group says the backlogged welding projects are a minor blip in the overall profitability picture, then all your proof will be "beside the point."

TIP 192: Create Immediacy to Generate an Emotional Reaction

If you are a single adult reading a news story about a teenager killed on a motorcycle because he wasn't wearing a safety helmet, you may feel sorry, shake your head, and continue reading. However, if you just bought your 18-year-old a motorcycle and had an argument with him or her about the importance of wearing a safety helmet, you probably will tune in a little closer to the statistics to find out how you can convince your son or daughter to wear a helmet.

Bring your presentation issue as close to home as possible. Make your audience see, hear, touch, and feel the situation.

If the members of your management team hear about the low unemployment rate on the news, they will have a general awareness of the difficulty of retaining competent employees. However, if you cite the 38 percent increase in employee turnover at your Detroit plant, adding that the company's rehiring and retraining costs hit the half-million mark for the past year, these managers will quickly see the urgency of the employee-retention problem.

Whether you are talking about money, management, or marital problems, appeal to your listeners emotionally. Then supply the information to help them justify their decisions logically.

TIP 193: Source Information Specifically

How much faith do you put in product testimonials signed by first names only, with no organization? Specific sourcing adds credibility. We have all become wary of the political reporter's catchall phrase "unidentified sources claim . . ." that renders the information debatable, unverifiable, and useless for all except the evening news.

TIP 194: Know When *Not* to Quote an Expert

Certainly, experts lend authority to your persuasive effort. If you quote the plant manager about the efficiency of the equipment, followed by the engineering operator, and then a leading manufacturing rep in the industry, they may all pile on great data to help you make your point more persuasive.

Likewise, motivating employees to become leaders, think creatively, embrace change, and provide better customer service requires moments of inspiration. One or two pithy quotations can sell an idea and motivate audiences to action. However, 10 or 12 quotations dropped into a presentation can drown any breath of fresh air from the speaker.

Avoid quoting so many experts that you diminish your own authority.

TIP 195: Ask for Small Commitments Along the Way

People like to think they behave consistently. Once you ask them to make a small decision, they are more likely to agree to a larger one. For example, early in your presentation, you may talk about a key problem in your organization and identify the wasted dollars attributed to the problem. Ask for agreement from your listeners about the problem. Then later when you ask for a decision to solve the problem, they will be more likely to agree because human nature dictates that we behave consistently with earlier commitments (that there is a problem that needs to be solved).

Never, however, use this principle in a manipulative way involving unimportant questions or decision points. When audiences feel manipulated with an "in your face," aggressive request for agreement every couple of minutes, they will offer resistance rather than resolve.

TIP 196: Never Underestimate the "Like" Factor

Have you ever noticed that the grocery sacker begins to talk to you about the weather, sports, or whatever as he or she pushes your grocery cart to your car? Or that the cab driver asks if you are in town on business or pleasure and where you are from and how your flight was? Or how often the waiter at the restaurant comments on your cute kids? And then have noticed how much bigger the tip you give to these service people than to those who are sullen, grumpy, or reserved?

It should come as no surprise that when your audience likes you, they are more likely to be persuaded about what you have to say.

TIP 197: Ask for a Suspension of Judgment

When you know your listeners likely will be biased against what you have to say, admit the situation—not bluntly, of course, but diplomatically. Chances are good that your listeners will give you a fair hearing. It is amazing what people will do when you simply acknowledge and ask.

TIP 198: Listen to What Your Audience Wants to Hear

According to the French philosopher Voltaire, "The road to the heart is the ear." Communication is always a two-way process—even when you are presenting. When your audience members interrupt to speak up, listen up. They will give great clues as to what is behind their statements. Once you have identified their interests, needs, fears, and concerns, you can address and reassure them.

TIP 199: Use Straightforward Language, Not Overblown Exaggerations and Vague Claims

"Ninety percent of our orders last year came from repeat buyers" is much more persuasive than "Belco can meet all your hardware and software needs."

TIP 200: Leave Out Limp Language that Screams "Loophole"

Buyers of ideas know to beware when they hear words like these: "This *may* be appropriate in your situation." "I'll *try* to get the survey and report completed by next month." "This diagnostic testing *usually* works." "*Most* of the users in our department find this feature well worth the money." Limp language says to the audience, "I'm not really sure and do not want to go out on a limb with a definite statement that you can hold me to."

Disclaimers and qualifiers yell "loophole, loophole" in the minds of listeners. Of course, you never state something outright that you cannot support. However, neither should you get in the habit of filling your presentation with disclaimers such as, "Guarantees are subject to change without notice" or "Delivery schedules may vary, of course, depending on peak workloads."

TIP 201: Serve a Fresh, Not Canned, Sound

Sound has more to do with perception than language—that is, words that sound artificial, memorized, or canned. When phrases start to roll off your tongue, you are in danger of sounding too slick. Few prospects (external buyers of your products and services or internal buyers of your ideas) are persuaded by phoniness. They prefer sincerity that comes across in fresh, not stale, syntax and word choices.

8

Giving a Good Story a Fighting Chance

As I grow older, I become more and more of a Marxist—Groucho. That is, when you have lived two-thirds of your life, you know the value of a good joke.   KAREN DECROW

Humor brings insight and tolerance.
                                                              AGNES REPPLIER

The essence of humor is that it should be unexpected, that it should embody an element of surprise, that it should startle us out of that reasonable gravity, which, after all, must be our habitual frame of mind.   AGNES REPPLIER

Humor comes from self-confidence. There's an aggressive element to wit.   RITA MAE BROWN

The universe is made of stories, not of atoms.
                                                          MURIEL RUKEYSER

Stories grab attention the way no other technique can. Your anecdote may be serious, sad, humorous, enlightening, or inspiring. It may serve as proof that a situation exists in your organization, an example of what excellent organizations do to lead the industry, the epitome of innovation, a thought-

105

provoking "war story" from one of your front-line employees, or merely a momentary inspiration.

Even with a serious point, humor generally helps. However, it is a good idea to develop some healthy humor habits while you still have a day job.

Humor may involve a light approach to a scene, a witty offhand comment, or a self-deprecating story. Your purpose is not to bring down the house with wildly funny stories; the audience does not expect Jay Leno or David Letterman. A lighthearted approach in making your point will be sufficient and memorable.

A humorous story may be the only part of your presentation the audience remembers. This fact has hit me hard several times over the years. For instance, in our business-writing workshops for corporate clients, our instructors make the point that a careless change in verb tense and mood can alter the meaning of a document completely. For reinforcement, we show a 30-second video clip and close with a brief story about a frequent airline comment to passengers. Several years after attending a particular workshop, a participant saw me in the building lobby when I returned to do another workshop for his organization and commented on the value of the training program to his career.

I was about to pat myself on the back about all the valuable concepts that he probably remembered and was using daily—things like how to structure documents, tips on getting started quickly, and tips for managing high-volume e-mail. Then he added this comment: "Yeah, I'll never forget that story about the flight attendant always saying, "We would like to thank you for flying with us today." And then he quoted the exact punch line from my story of three years earlier. (Now, while I agree that the one-liner works in a way that is truly memorable, it unfortunately illustrated one of the least important concepts of the entire workshop.)

It does, however, prove my point: Stories pack power. Humor anchors key points. Humor makes your message memorable.

Another story I use creates audience identification. I describe the time that I arrived for a 6 A.M. breakfast meeting so tired and rushed that, without realizing it, I brushed my teeth and put on my makeup in the men's rest room. Sharing self-deprecating personal stories can provide an excellent source of original humor that everyone can relate to. Audiences appreciate your candor in revealing your mistakes to make a point. Just be careful that the stories are humorous rather than boastful.

If there is one place where humor can add a distinctive flavor to a presentation, it is in the business arena. If you want to stand out in a customer's memory or during a board member's evaluation of your new management philosophy, add a touch of humor. Slanting your story to your audience—their point of view and their mood—adds to the impact.

When done well, a humorous story adds an element of class and distinction.

TIP 202: Know Your Reason for Using a Story

To illustrate a point, to entertain, or to build common ground with your audience—identifying your purpose will make your selection much easier. You also will understand the length of time you should devote to telling it and the effort that should go into telling it well. Never use a $100 story in a three-minute time slot to make a nickel point.

TIP 203: Set Up the Anecdote in an Intriguing Way

Not: "Let me tell you about a manager in our Miami office."
But: "Managers sometimes exhibit their greatest leadership skills when they make a mistake. This was the case in our Miami office last quarter when. . . ."

TIP 204: Choose Relevant, Appropriate Details

It is tempting to talk while you think. Don't. Either work out your story by talking it aloud until you perfect it, or write the story and then edit out the garbage. Ask yourself with each word, phrase, and sentence: Does it add to the mood? Does it create the scene? Is this detail necessary to move the story forward and make the point? Weed out trivial details that detract or add only length.

TIP 205: Prefer Scene to Narrative

Recreate the movie scene, add the dialogue, and step into the story as a character, if necessary, to breathe life into the telling.

Not this narrative: "I had a terrible experience the last time I visited my doctor's office. The receptionist was surly and kept scolding me and other patients for "noise" as if we were children. Customer service certainly isn't what it used to be."

But this scene: "I'm not one easily persuaded to see a doctor. And I get particularly upset about the lack of customer service in most medical offices. But last fall when my fever reached 103 degrees, I finally stagger into my internist's office, dehydrated, dizzy, and green from lunch. And the receptionist pushes a clipboard toward me and growls, 'You'll need to complete this.' So I'm sitting there with all the paperwork piled in my lap, scrawling in the blanks: Name, rank, serial number, referring physician, address of hairdresser, IQ. And the clipboard breaks and shoots the spring in the handle across the room into the water cooler with a loud zing. Then this lady beside me starts to sneeze and wheeze so loud that it catches the attention of the toddler with measles next to her. So then the toddler starts to screech at his lung's capacity, 'Mommy, what's she doing?' About this time, the receptionist opens her cubicle window again and says, 'Could I ask you people to keep down the noise please. There are sick people in here.' "

TIP 206: Look for Places to Exaggerate the Details for Effect and Humor

Consider the scene in the preceding tip—specifically the line about completing the paperwork and how loud the toddler screamed. The essence of a story should stay true. However, look for details that increase the humor index.

As a storyteller, when you get hung up staying with the actual details (Did the hotel agent have only three rooms with a king bed or only three rooms period? Was it a migraine headache or just a bad headache? Was it the last plane leaving the terminal or just the last plane with that airline?), the audience also can get confused along the way. When there seems to be a contradiction, they focus on substantiating the validity of the actual incident rather than the key message you are illustrating. With obvious exaggeration, they relax and understand that the incident is generally true and that the whole situation is meant to convey a general point.

Exaggerate to help your audience focus on the message rather than reality.

TIP 207: Ensure That Every Story Has a Beginning, a Middle, and an End

See the scene in Tip 205 about the surly receptionist in the medical office. You will notice that although the story is less than 60 seconds long when delivered, it has a definite beginning, middle, and end. Without all three, your listeners feel as though you are leaving something incomplete. Granted, you do not have to complete the entire story at one time. You may move the story along during an entire presentation to make several key points during your talk.

TIP 208: Select Stories with a Universal Truth

As human beings, we are more alike than different. This makes it much easier for you as a presenter to ensure that your anecdotes will have the same meaning to all listeners. Yes, your listeners may experience a truth in different intensities, but they should all understand the point. Otherwise, you have done nothing more than create an "inside joke" that some will catch and others will miss, creating a barrier rather than a bond.

TIP 209: Select Heroes with Which Your Participants Can Identify

If you are talking to front-line people, use anecdotes about front-line people—not chief executive officers (CEOs), franchise owners, or stock analysts. If you are presenting a motivational talk to ask people to get involved in a charitable project, select an anecdote about the single mom who has a child with leukemia and needs help with the rent rather than about an ex-convict who needs tuition aid until he finds a job.

TIP 210: Make Your Heroes Wear Both Black and White Hats

The heroes of your anecdotes do not have to do everything right, have perfect careers, made all the correct choices, and have pleasing personalities all the time—they just need to be real and make your point. People accept imperfection and expect reality on the road to possibility thinking.

TIP 211: Remember That Heroes Do Not Necessarily Have to Win or Save the Day

We learn from failure as well as from success—sometimes more so. The hero should be human and sympathetic. That is, we have to like someone and identify with their feelings, hopes, dreams, fears, and goals before we can learn from them. Otherwise, when we hear of their experiences, situations, and feats, our reaction may be, "Ho-hum. So what does that have to do with me?"

TIP 212: Perfect Facial Expression, Voice Tone, and Body Language to Be an Essential Part of the Story

In the same way that both content and delivery work together to make your entire presentation either dynamic or distasteful, a story and its delivery work together to create the total impact. A raised eyebrow, a haughty tone, or a shrug of the shoulders can carry—or reverse—your point.

TIP 213: Let the Punch Line Stand on Its Own

If you have to explain the punch line, it does not work. Play with it until it does. Sometimes the substitution of one key word will make the difference between a laugh and blank stare, between an "aaahhh-haaa" and a "huh?" Practice the punch line and the punch word until others understand it. If they do not, delete it rather than explain it.

TIP 214: Don't Rush the Laugh Lines or the Pregnant Pauses

Standing silent while an audience responds takes courage. Such pauses may be the longest of your career. However, if you rush through them, the audience will take their cue from you and assume that you did not want or intend for them to respond audibly. Their nonresponse then destroys your confidence to try additional stories in the remaining sections of your presentation. As a result, your delivery gets dryer and dryer. The presentation spirals downward to disappointment.

TIP 215: Remember, the Longer the Story, the Funnier the Punch Line Needs to Be

Attention spans are short. Lengthy stories can lead to big expectations. They end in disappointment with a poorly delivered or less-than-hilarious punch line.

TIP 216: Avoid a Big Buildup That Sets Up Disappointment

Inexperienced speakers warn, "Here comes a joke," with a lead-in like, "That reminds me of the story about . . ." or "I've got a great story that makes a point about X. It's so funny. You're not going to believe what this customer really said to me. But I want to tell you about this situation just to illustrate my point about the type of demands our customers are placing on us these days. It's hilarious. I couldn't believe he really did this. This guy was really crazy. Just irate. Cursing. Yelling. The whole thing was so ridiculous. Here's what happened. This customer calls up on our support line and. . . ."

With such a long buildup, the typical audience reaction after you tell the anecdote will be, "That wasn't such a great story. And it wasn't so funny."

Just get into the story and then make your point. The audience will let you know if it was funny or not.

TIP 217: Perfect Your Timing

One word botched, mumbled, or out of order can sink the ship. Practice your delivery.

Thank you for your attention. Some of you are
obviously into assertive listening.
RICH'S CURRENT HUMOR NEWSLETTER

Our After Dinner keynoter comes to us from a
humble beginning. He started out as an After
Snack speaker.
RICH'S CURRENT HUMOR NEWSLETTER

Most of the speakers you'll hear today constitute
a sort of who's who in the industry. I'm more
in the category of who's he.
MICHAEL IAPOCE

TIP 218: Rework Your Story Until Perfected

Changing a single word, adding one specific detail, or changing a person's name can be the difference between confusion and clarity, a laugh and a ho-hum, retention and oblivion.

TIP 219: Never Use Unrelated Humor

Make your humor an integral part of your presentation. Even if it is your favorite joke, a canned joke will sound contrived and out of place, distracting your listeners from your point rather than reinforcing it. Instead, integrate the humor with the message. Make the point. Tell the story. Restate the point.

TIP 220: Rehearse Your Stories and One-Liners "Off Broadway"

Before you use an anecdote "live" in a presentation, make sure that it works. And the best way to do this is to see how others react as you tell it. Tell it to your family and friends. Tell it at a cocktail party. Tell it at work in the cafeteria. Where do people laugh? At what details do people's expressions change? Where do their eyes grow larger? Where are they shocked? Amused? Appalled? On the next telling, play up those parts. Create more suspense. Add more dialogue, less narration.

You will generally improve your delivery with each telling. Sometimes people laugh at things you did not think were the funny part—and vice versa. It is better to know this before telling the story "for real" in your presentation to drive home a key point.

TIP 221: Don't Try Humor on a Tough Crowd

Occasionally you run into audience members who seem to pride themselves on being unresponsive. Their body language—if not their words beforehand—wants you to know that they are not easily swayed, that they are *not* inclined to think that you are witty, that the subject is to be taken lightly, that your approach is amusing. In short, they want you to know they have "heard it all."

Unless you are extremely confident in front of an unresponsive group, the sooner you receive the message they are sending, the better.

TIP 222: Retain Your Composure When a Story Bombs

Sometimes it is not the failed humor but the sagging confidence that damages a speaker's impact during a presentation. Any speaker, no matter how polished, occasionally meets a group that does not respond to a specific story, to a particular type of humor, or to any humor at all.

When your humor does not work, be prepared to make your point seriously. If you have delivered your punch line and no one laughs during the pause, simply continue with your point. "In much more serious circumstances, folks, our budget can't stand . . ." or "No matter what your perspective—lighthearted or serious—the process needs to be changed in that . . ." or "Fortunately, most people have a more serious view of leadership than the Mr. Andrews of my story."

And there are always favorite "saver" lines that professional speakers use in such circumstances: "Look, if I'm going to have to explain these to you, I could maybe do a diagram for that purpose" or "You in the back laughing, would you stand up and explain it to the rest of them" or: "[Call someone's name in the audience that everyone knows], that's the last time I'm going to use one of your stories."

TIP 223: Remember That the Larger the Crowd, the Easier the Laugh

For some reason, people tend to feel "safer" trying humor with a smaller group. In reality, your opportunity for success will be greater with a larger crowd. Because a laugh is a shared experience, in a small group of seven, people are more guarded with an audible response. They sometimes fear laughing "alone," so they sometimes prefer to chuckle "under their breath." When the group numbers 500, they feel "lost in a crowd" and don't think their chuckle will be noticed or spotted.

Laughter becomes contagious—a lighthearted titter typically becomes contagious and generates more laughter. So never fear to use planned humor simply because you have a larger than expected crowd.

9

Visuals That Support, Not Sabotage

Multimedia? As far as I'm concerned, it's reading with the radio on!   RORY BREMMER

No typo ever goes away. It just moves somewhere else.   HORTON'S LAWS

This thing called statistics was the worst thing that was invented; it's the curse of the world. We wouldn't know how bad the others were doing if we didn't have statistics.   WILL ROGERS

Visuals can add glitz, glamour, or garbage. They bombard us daily. With visuals, TV commercials and magazine ads try to sell us products and services. *USA TODAY* and *The Wall Street Journal* deliver economic, financial, and statistical news using icons symbolizing oilrigs, moneybags, and attaché cases. Weather forecasters predict tomorrow's conditions on colored maps. Flight attendants demonstrate (rather than simply describe) proper emergency procedures during air travel. Restaurants include photos of their offerings on their menus; others send around dessert carts that tempt us with the real thing. Why all the visual stimuli? Two reasons—retention and impact.

Consider how your own brain works in the following situations: When friends give directions to their homes, do they usually write out a step-by-step description of the route or draw you a map? Which do you remember better—faces or names? Do you prefer to listen to radio or watch TV when you are at home? Would you rather listen to recordings of your favorite

Do You Draw a Map or Write Out Travel Procedures?

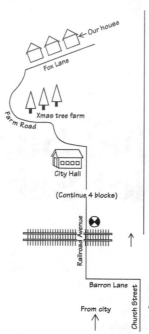

1. Go north on Church Street until you reach the white church.

2. Turn left on Barron Lane.

3. Turn right on Railroad Avenue and cross the railroad tracks.

4. Go on for a while and turn left onto Farm Road at City Hall.

5. On your right, you'll see a Christmas tree farm then you'll be at Fox Lane (right turn).

6. We're the third house on the left.

Visuals improve clarity and add impact.

artists or see them perform live? Which is more memorable to you when you go to a movie—the names on the movie credits as they roll across the screen or the opening action scene?

In today's environment, most audiences expect visuals—especially business audiences. If you are giving a presentation without them, be very sure you have a *brief* message, *intriguing* content, and a *captivating* delivery. Visuals clarify ideas, aid listener retention, and create audience interest that is difficult to generate any other way.

People learn in different ways. Some learn more by what they see, others learn better by what they hear, and still others by what they feel or experience. However, no one would disagree that using all three techniques increases retention and impact dramatically.

University studies suggest the same results. At the University of Wisconsin, researchers determined that retention improves up to 200 percent when visual aids are used in teaching vocabulary. Studies at Harvard and Columbia revealed that presentations with visuals improve student retention by 14 to 38 percent over presentations without visuals. Studies at the University of Pennsylvania's Wharton School of Business demonstrated that the time needed to make a point could be reduced by up to 40 percent when visuals accompany an oral presentation. In addition, these studies showed that audiences rated presenters who used visuals more favorably than presenters who did not. Specifically, the audiences judged these presenters to be better prepared and more persuasive than those not using visuals.

Presentations magazine and 3M Corporation sponsored a study to measure the effectiveness of multimedia presentations specifically. The study gauged the reactions of audiences to the same information presented with three different kinds of visual support: electronic slides, overhead transparencies, and text only.

Here is what they discovered about information recall, comprehension, and fact recognition: Multimedia presentations were more successful in helping listeners recognize facts, slightly superior for recall of all types of information generally, and markedly superior in helping audiences actually comprehend what the presenter was explaining.

Audiences also were asked to judge the overall effectiveness of the presenter and the presentation quality with the same three kinds of visual support. As expected, text-only presentations required the most from listeners. They had to be engaged to read the text—if they got the information at all. There was no one to explain or summarize the information to them.

When judging presenter effectiveness, multimedia presentations proved to be superior to overhead-transparency presentations. Of course, when information was presented by text only, there was no presenter to be judged.

Finally, in considering overall effectiveness of presentation quality, audiences again rated multimedia presentations markedly higher than overhead-transparency or text-only presentations.

Lawyers use physical evidence and exhibits, engineers use maps and mock-ups, retailers use catalogs and samples, doctors use x-rays and charts, dentists use molds and drawings, and stock analysts use graphics and printouts. Whatever the profession or presentation purpose, the results will be more dramatic with visuals.

GENERAL GUIDELINES

TIP 224: Identify Your Purpose in Using Any Specific Visual

Visuals take time and may cost money, and their use has been known to cause mishaps or confusion. However, the results can be well worth the effort because they can command attention, aid retention, make complex concepts clear, eliminate the need for words, add variety and pizzazz to your delivery style, and underscore your preparation for your audience. Just be sure that you know why you are making the effort and using your own and your audience's time to show a visual. In short, make the visual serve your purpose.

TIP 225: Use a Visual for "Shock Value" When Presenting New Data

Words are usually adequate for narratives, anecdotes, or humor if the speaker is energetic and creative enough to carry the point with enthusiasm and colorful phrasing. However, visuals have the impact required for presenting new data. With statistics, lists, trends, and similar information not easily grasped, analyzed, or retained, visuals provide the initial shock, aid interpretation, and then serve as reference for later study and comparisons.

TIP 226: Never Use Visuals to "Cover" for Problems

Presenters have used visuals to cover for a multitude of problems—to serve as "notes" to jog their memory about the next point, to fill time in case they run out of something meaningful to say, or to give them something to do with their hands such as holding a remote mouse. Using visuals indiscriminately decreases their effectiveness when you really need them.

TIP 227: Limit the Number of Visuals

Watch for thoughts like, "As long as I'm preparing slides, I may as well do 25 as 15." Any technique—even the most creative slides—can get monotonous. As a rule of thumb, your presentation should average no more than one visual per minute. *Average* is a deceiving word here, however. For example, during a presentation to a group of proposal writers, I may use three slides in five minutes to present examples of unclear documents. On the other hand, I may use no visual at all for 20 minutes during a keynote address on life balance or communication.

Vary number and selection based on topic and purpose. Less is more.

TIP 228: Don't Let Visuals Dominate

"Don't become an usher in your own theater," warns speaker Ron Hoff. In other words, do not let your media upstage you. Your purpose is not to guide your audience from visual to visual. If this is your approach, you may as well prepare bound sets of visuals and distribute them to your audience members for self-study.

You should dominate; your visuals should *support.* Depending on the types of visuals you use—slides, handouts, flipcharts—consider setting up your projector screens or easels at the side of the room so that you retain your place at "center stage."

TIP 229: Avoid Visual After Visual of "Laundry Lists"

The next worst visual—second only to a full page of text projected on the screen—is a bulleted list of single words or topics. After a while, such charts all begin to look like your grocery list. Consider how you can convey your ideas through a more creative visual than words alone.

Presenters are tempted to use such visuals because they provide an outline to speak from without the audience seeing any notes. But using visuals containing only words defeats your purpose. Even when displayed in a clever way, words are not visual. Photographs, diagrams, art, line graphs, and cartoons are. This is not to say that you should never use a text-only

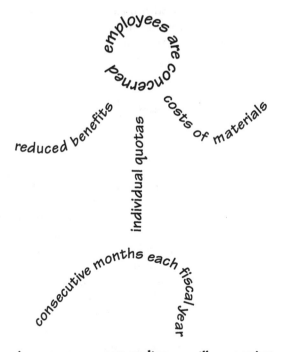

Are you sure your audience will recognize this as a picture of Harry Jones?

visual. If you do, however, be sure to supplement it with other visuals that "fill in" what's missing from the collection of words.

TIP 230: Select Visuals Appropriate to the Concept

Real objects or simulated models best demonstrate operating procedures or processes. Enlarged photos or line drawings best illustrate internal workings of equipment. Line graphs best show trends (as opposed to exact numbers). Bar charts best illustrate high-low comparisons. Flowcharts best exhibit interactive processes or the passage of time. Pictures or cartoons best illustrate concepts.

TIP 231: Incorporate Variety

If you have decided to use one visual medium for the majority of a presentation, consider adding others simply for a change of pace. In our one- or two-day training presentations, on average, our facilitators use six types of visual aids: multimedia slides, video clips, flipcharts, handouts of case studies and other exercises, demonstration objects and props, and reference books. Then, within each of these visual categories, we vary the use of text, cartoons, symbols, diagrams, and photos.

In my keynotes, I may use cartoons, photos, and props with the audience or, occasionally, no visuals at all.

TIP 232: Make Visuals Attractive

You may think that this goes without saying, but I recently attended a meeting where 22 representatives of a multibillion-dollar company presented their ideas visually. Some used slick, commercially prepared slides and videos. Three used transparencies of typed text. And these were people who make presentations for a living!

This is not to say that presenters should spend a fortune having their visuals produced commercially. While commercial visuals look great, they may convey the wrong impression to a prospective buyer—for instance, that you have plenty of money to waste and do not need the business. To a boss or executive committee, they may say that you have way too much time on your hands. "Canned" visuals also may convey the idea that you have not taken time to tailor your presentation to your audience.

Attractive and *expensive* aren't necessarily synonymous. Presentation software has put quality visuals within the range of almost everyone's budget and ability. By creating your own, you can customize them easily and quickly for specific audiences. Sloppy visuals convey lack of forethought and a perception of shoddy work—issues of concern to both buyers and bosses.

TIP 233: Proofread Carefully

Misspellings, typos, inconsistencies in wording and design, and broken lettering can be major distractions. A misspelling interrupts the listeners' thought processes, causing them to wonder, "Should I point this out? I wonder if the speaker is aware of this? Does she not recognize the error? Doesn't he care?" Such errors damage an image of professionalism and leave the impression of hurried, inadequate preparation.

Always allow a cool-off period between the production of your visuals and your practice time so that you can review your visuals with a fresh eye. It is also a good idea to have others proofread them for inconsistencies and errors that you may have missed.

TIP 234: Have an Alternate Game Plan for Getting Your Information Across Without Visuals

You never know when some unforeseen occurrence makes using your planned visuals impossible—from a power outage, to the discovery that your handout has two typos, to a client's remark that he or she does not "have time" for you to set up any audiovisual (AV) aids.

And then there's the more unusual situation: A colleague recently prepared a talk for a group of 15 people on communication in foreign cultures. When she arrived for the presentation, she discovered that two of the 15 participants were blind. She changed her goal to making the talk meaningful and interesting without using visuals—a challenge any presenter would do well to consider.

TIP 235: Coordinate Your Delivery Details with the Visual

Almost every visual aid requires practice for smooth manipulation and staging. If possible, practice in the room where you will give the presentation. Study the angles to determine where you will stand so that you can see your notes or outline without blocking your audience's view.

Decide beforehand where you will stand as you display each visual. When using an overhead projector, will you stand to the left of the screen, or will you need to be near the projector base to write on the transparency? Will you need to move the VCR monitor to the middle of the conference room during the video clip, or will everyone be able to see the screen at an angle? Does the built-in multimedia system have rear-screen projection? If so, where are the controls? If you use a lectern for holding your notes, will you need a page of that information as you move closer to the flipchart or your laptop?

In practicing with visuals such as slides, videos, or multimedia where the equipment is located away from the stage area, you may discover that you need an assistant. Making this discovery beforehand can prevent embarrassing foul-ups.

However, do not let the fact that you need to move around to different locations in the room cause undue concern. Movement adds energy to your delivery and keeps the audience alert. Physically moving from one AV aid to another brings closure to an idea or activity and gives the audience time to make a transition in their thinking.

When you are summoned to the boss's office to give a spur-of-the-moment update on a project in a sit-down situation, you may not have time to locate a projector. A quick change of plans about the kind of visual to use—a transparency turned into a handout or a slideshow directly from your laptop—may be in order.

Whichever visuals you select, position them as if the desktop or conference table is your stage. When holding a handout toward your audience, position it right side up for them, and use a pen or pencil as your pointer. Put visuals out of sight when you finish discussing them.

TIP 236: Present the Visual, and Then Pause

When first displaying a visual, pause to give the audience a couple of moments to take it in. If you start speaking immediately, they will miss your first few words while previewing your display. After this uninterrupted preview, they will switch gears and begin listening to you again as you elaborate and build your point.

TIP 237: Talk to the Audience, Not the Visuals

Visuals are for the audience, not the presenter. Never face your visuals while talking or, worse yet, read them to your audience. Know your material well enough to be able to maintain eye contact while elaborating on the key points using your own words. The visual is the beginning point, not the end.

TIP 238: Stand to the Left of the Visuals from the Audience's Viewpoint

You undoubtedly will be moving around during your presentation and not standing "at attention" beside your visuals for the duration of your presentation. However, when you come to a segment of your presentation where you plan to use several text-heavy or data-filled visuals closely together, stand to the left of the screen. Because people read text from left to right, their eyes will naturally return to you after they have finished reviewing the visual. This is particularly important if you will be referring them back and forth several times to the visual, such as pointing out data on a chart as you add elaboration after each reference.

TIP 239: Make Your Audience Move

Use your entire "stage area" for your visuals. For example, in a conference room, you may have a flipchart to the right side of the room, your laptop and screen to the left side of the room, and your stack of printouts at the back. Your audience will turn with you as you move around the room, sliding their chairs or shifting their positions to gain a better view.

This movement, however slight, keeps them more alert and reduces the tension of sitting in one spot and facing one direction for long periods of time. Movement on the part of the audience is beneficial, not detrimental, to your presentation.

TIP 240: Select Your Visuals with Several Criteria in Mind

On occasion, habit becomes an inhibitor to superior choice. When selecting visuals, consider the culture and expectations of the group you will be addressing, cost, availability of equipment, production time, room size, audience size, seating arrangements, and lighting conditions.

TIP 241: Set Your Screen Up So That It's Off-Center

You yourself should be center stage in front of your audience. Your group came to hear you—not to see your slideshow. Otherwise, you could have e-mailed them your handouts or your slides. When you stand to the side and place your visuals center stage, the danger is that you become only a slide narrator.

In most rooms, a screen set diagonally across the corner of the room works well, depending on the seating arrangement.

TIP 242: Open and Close Your Presentation Without a Visual in Sight

As you begin and end, the focus should be on you, the speaker—not on your visual support.

DESIGN GUIDELINES FOR MULTIMEDIA

TIP 243: Cut the Clutter

Avoid text, data, and art that does not clearly relate to the key concept. Do not bombard your audience with statistics and numbers that dilute rather than strengthen your main points. Listeners need to grasp the key concepts (such as, "Our costs have risen 40 percent"); they will pick up the specifics from your handout and can mull them over later. Also, make sure that your font style and size are uniform; both should contribute to ease of reading, not create visual clutter. Adequate white space also helps viewers differentiate between main ideas and supporting ideas and makes comparisons easy. Finally, make sure animation aids understanding rather than distracts. Just because you can easily make lines and objects swirl, dance, and flash does not mean they should.

TIP 244: Limit Each Slide to One Major Concept

One purpose of a visual is to simplify complex data. If listeners have to study the visual to understand it, the visual misses the target.

TIP 245: Use Parallel Structure

Equal ideas should get equal structure. If you use phrases in your bulleted lists, they should match—either all verb phrases, all noun phrases, or all adjective phrases. Bulleted lists should not be mixed—part phrases and part sentences. In addition to being grammatically incorrect, scrambled, unparallel lists take longer to read.

TIP 246: Use No More Than Six Lines of Text and No More Than Six Words per Line

Crowded visuals make your points difficult to read at best. Include only key words and phrases. Fill in the complete idea with your elaboration.

TIP 247: Use a Minimum Font Size of 24 Points for Text and 40 Points for Titles

Anything smaller will be unreadable unless you are giving a sit-down presentation from your laptop to one or two people.

TIP 248: Use a Sans Serif Typeface to Increase Readability

Serif typefaces are those with curls and swirls at the bottoms and tops of letters. Although they look fancy for wedding and party invitations and graduation and birth announcements, they do nothing for readability.

TIP 249: Use Both Upper- and Lowercase— Rather than All Uppercase

Text in all uppercase is more difficult to read than using both upper- and lowercase. Our eyes are used to seeing a capital letter to know when to start a new sentence and a new thought. All uppercase text slows readers down.

TIP 250: Use Appropriate Color Contrast

The starker the contrast between the text color and the background color, the more readable the text. White text on a dark-green background pops out, whereas black text on a dark-green background may be unreadable. Most presenters notice such problems for their primary text but fail to consider secondary words and phrases such as those on labels or column headings or in photographs or drawings. Whatever text appears on the visual, the audience will assume they need to read it. Color it so that they can.

TIP 251: Use Color to Attract Attention, to Emphasize, and to Link Similar Ideas

Rather than simply adding color because technology has made it possible to use 256 shades, choose for a specific effect: to link equivalent points, to create a mood, to improve readability, to highlight key ideas, and then to subordinate supporting detail.

Bold colors—such as blue, black, green, and purple—are good for primary ideas. Avoid light, iridescent colors that cannot be seen easily.

Subliminally reinforce your message with carefully selected color: Blue serves as the background color for the vast majority of all business presentations. It is the color of conservatism, credibility, tranquility, and trust.

Green also can be an excellent background or accent color. It is the color of interaction, envy, growth, prosperity, money, relaxation, and stability.

Red grabs attention and demands action. It is the color of both passion and pain and both loss and gain. Red can express eagerness, caution, danger, or hostility. Use it carefully so that you do not send a mixed message—for example, with accountants in talking about your financial performance!

Purple works well as both a background and an accent color, depending on whether you use a dark or light shade. Purple is the color of royalty, spirituality, vision, dreams, and humor.

Yellow serves well for text or accents against a dark background. It is the color of energy, action, cheerfulness, enthusiasm, optimism, and warmth. However, in surveys of popularity, yellow is the least favorite of all colors.

Black works well as a text, background, or accent color. It is bold, clean, sophisticated, and final.

White works best as a text color on a dark background. If you use it as a background color, you will need to add accent colors to make it come alive. It symbolizes a "clean slate," purity, naivety, neutrality, wisdom, simplicity, or "no frills."

Tailor your colors to your audience's biases, experiences, and expectations.

Visit the Web site *www.colormatters.com* for more than you will ever want to know about colors and slide presentations.

TIP 252: Limit Text Colors to Two or Three in Any Specific Presentation

Besides text and art clutter, there's also color clutter. To please the eye and to emphasize and organize ideas, color is a plus. But consider it primarily an accent—for icons, titles, art, and other graphic elements. Two colors are good; a third can highlight; a fourth usually clutters.

Using too many colors in one presentation creates a "cartoonish" effect. Use the cartoon effect with purpose—to create humor or a light approach. When your intention is to be serious, stay with a select, stylish color palette.

TIP 253: Select Dark Text Against a Lighter Background When You Cannot Control the Lighting in the Room

This text and background combination provides maximum contrast and readability when you do not know in what setting you will be showing your slides and cannot always control the lighting. The same situation holds true if you are using a low-lumen projector that does not provide as much light: Select the darker text, accents, and graphics.

TIP 254: Select Light Text Against a Darker Background When You Can Control the Lighting and Can Fade the Lights on the Screen

This text and background combination provides maximum contrast and readability when you have complete control over the setting and are using a high-lumen projector. You can fade the house lights in front of the screen so that the slides do not appear "washed out."

TIP 255: Select Subtle Background Templates That Match Your Objective, Content, and Culture

Is your group conservative, futuristic, or avant garde? Will you be speaking to shareholders, front-line cashiers, or customers? Do you want them to save or spend? Do you want them to feel annoyed at the activists or pleased at your proposal? With so many predesigned templates at our fingertips, it is tempting to select one that swirls, shimmers, and shakes with colors and graphics—just because we can. When this is the case, they become more than a background—they often overpower the key message of the slide.

TIP 256: Include Blank, Logo, or Theme Slides as the First and Last

These slides allow you to bring up your slideshow and make any necessary adjustments without early arrivers seeing your real first slide of information.

TIP 257: Select a Short Music Cut Relating to a Key Point Rather Than Continual Background Music

Continual background music detracts from and sometimes overpowers both your visual and your message. Less is more. Cute can turn to annoying quickly.

TIP 258: Vary Types of Data Charts Shown Consecutively

Rather than four pie charts in a row, try to arrange your information so that you can break up the monotony. Of course, you always want to select a visual appropriate to the concept. So never vary the visual at the expense of miscommunicating the message.

TIP 259: Title Each Visual with Informative Headings

Imagine strolling past your TV and catching a glimpse of action on the screen while the volume is turned down. Chances are, after a few seconds, you will be able to figure out what's happening. Likewise, your visuals should be complete enough to stand alone. Use either an informative caption or a title to convey the key point to listeners who may have "tuned out" momentarily to your elaboration.

TIP 260: Break Down Large Sections of Slides with Unique Titles

It is not unusual to see slide A titled, "Marketing Plans for Next Year," slide B entitled, "Marketing Plans for New Product Lines," slide C titled, "Marketing Campaign for New Products," and slide D titled, "Marketing—Upcoming Plans for New Products." Even if these slides contain a smaller "heading" inside the slide, the primary title is wasted because they all say virtually the same thing.

Instead, cut to the chase. Title each slide with your key point *about that visual* rather than repeating the same global concept from slide to slide.

TIP 261: Label All Axes and Columns on Charts and Graphs

Presenters typically argue that their graphs are self-explanatory without labels. They rarely are. And even if listeners eventually figure them out, visuals are intended to help audiences grasp complex ideas *quickly*. Labels save time, not to mention improving clarity.

TIP 262: Use Vertical Lines for the Strongest Emphasis

Arrange headings so that the major classifications for ultimate comparison will be in vertical columns, not horizontal rows.

TIP 263: Express Fractions as Decimals in All Charts and Graphs

Decimals increase clarity. Prefer decimal points for precision when the fractional number is significant. Rounded numbers are easier to recall.

TIP 264: Use Standard Symbols and Abbreviations

Check a standard dictionary or technical glossary. You may be surprised to discover that *lb* stands for the plural *pounds* without the *s*, that months is abbreviated as *mo* not *mos*, or that your personal identification number is a *PIN* not a *P.I.N.*

TIP 265: Follow the Standard Rules of Capitalization

If you intend to emphasize something, either highlight it with an accent color, bold the entire word or select a different, larger font. Random capitalization makes reading difficult, creates grammatical errors, and causes clarity problem. (Is *Boston Airport* a different airport or a reference to Logan International? With the random capital *A*, the audience may wonder.)

TIP 266: Be Accurate and Precise in the Use of Scales of Measurement and in the Wording of Labels on Charts and Graphs

Use the same labels on your visuals as you intend to use in your elaboration. If you are going to talk about expenditures by quarter, do not create visuals that show expenses by month. Do the 20, 40, and 60 marks on the left side of the graph refer to product lines or percentages? Make sure that every scale has a label.

TIP 267: Use Round Numbers, Where Possible, on
Charts and Graphs

> For example, in stating years, drop the 20 and use only '03, '04, '05, '06, '07, '08, '09, and '10. Change the axis to thousands, when possible. Round 8.7947 to 8.8 unless precision to the fourth decimal point is meaningful. Approximate 48.2 percent to 48 percent except in presentations where exactness is a must.

TIP 268: Give the Sources of All Data Not Your Own

> Facts and ideas cannot be copyrighted. However, the unique expression of those ideas and facts can be. And certainly research, data, and information can be protected. Know and respect copyright laws to avoid placing yourself and your organization in serious legal difficulties.

TIP 269: Use Builds to Emphasize and to
Focus Attention

> Click only when you intend for your audience to read—no sooner. Otherwise, your visuals will compete with you.

TIP 270: Group Data and "Click-Ons" in Tiny Chunks
When You *Must* Show Complex Charts in One View

> One purpose of a visual is to help your audience grasp difficult information quickly. To flash a complex chart at them all at once defeats the purpose. Even if they eventually must see the chart all in one view to understand the big picture (for example, with an organizational chart or a diagram of a piece of equipment), you do not have to start out that way. And if you do have to start out that way for some reason, show the complete chart for a moment and then reverse the process: Begin your elaboration by taking away all groups of data but one and then adding the chunks back one by one as you explain each section.

TIP 271: Understand How Transitions and
Builds Affect the Pace

> The types of builds and transitions you decide to use will affect the pace of your presentation dramatically. Transitions that "fade through black" will

seem to take forever, whereas those that "appear," "fly in," "wipe right," or "wipe left" will feel faster.

Also consider the fact that when you decide to use a build rather than have all bullet points appear at once, you limit your options of how fast you can cover the material.

If all your bullet points appear at once and your time is short, you might say, "You'll notice the six steps we've taken this quarter to market product X. I'd like to take a couple of minutes to elaborate only on item four here." The audience will have an opportunity to skim for themselves all six steps. And then you can talk about the one most important item. Yet, if you had automated the bullets, you would have obligated yourself to talk a little more fully about each as you built the slide.

Transitions and builds affect pace. Consider both the pros and cons rather than letting the possibility of what you *can* do dictate what you *should* do.

TIP 272: Use the Same Transition Within Sections and Limit Transitions to No More than Three to Four Types per Presentation

Staying with one transitional effect—for example, vertical blinds or a wipe left—for a complete section of content helps the audience group your ideas mentally. When the transitions change, they understand that you have moved onto a new idea.

MULTIMEDIA SLIDES

TIP 273: Consider the Pros and Cons Carefully Before Deciding to Use Multimedia Slides

Pros

- Suitable for large audiences
- Professional appearance, indicating forethought
- Appealing range of colors, art, graphics, and typeface
- Ideal, precise reproduction of photos, graphics, or colored images
- Easy to use (with the push of a button or keystroke)
- Easy and inexpensive to update
- Transportable on laptop, removable disk, or CD or downloaded from the Web or transmittable electronically through e-mail

■ Immediately retrievable backup visuals from a database to respond to audience interest

Cons

■ Incompatibility problems with hardware at presentation site

■ Startup cost for projection equipment needed

■ Difficult to manipulate smoothly without practice (especially when moving back and forth in a presentation)

■ Noisy when using older projector models

TIP 274: Identify Sources for Purchasing Stock Imagery and Sounds

Here are several good sources you may want to check out:

www.BizPresenter.com—for PowerPoint templates, stock photography, and cartoons

www.gettyworks.com—for online image sites

www.arttoday.com—for stock photos and images

www.photostogo.com—for stock photos and images

www.cartoonresource.com—for existing or custom-designed cartoons

www.cartoonbank.com—for cartoons; this is the Web site of *New Yorker* magazine, with over 85,000 archived cartoons (sorted by categories) you can use for $35 each

www.creativemoonlighter.com—a network of freelancers to custom create cartoons, templates, drawings, and so forth

www.elance.com—a network of freelancers to custom create cartoons, templates, drawings, and so forth

www.tedgoff.com—business cartoons

www.photospin.com—free and for-fee photos

www.clipart.com—graphics, animations, and links to many other such Web sites

www.findsounds.com—lets you search the Web for sound effects and musical instrument samples

TIP 275: Know What Slide to Expect Next

Print a go-by sheet. You have several choices: Print out paper copies of individual slides. Or, print your slides six to a page with the number showing in each slide large enough so you can skip forward or backward quickly. Or, use the method your presentation software provides to print out only a list of slide titles and numbers. Or, use an electronic previewer.

TIP 276: Practice Manipulation of Planned and Backup Screens Ahead of Time

Know key slide numbers as well as tour guides know their museum routes—all the back doors, extra hallways, and shortcuts. Contrary to popular opinion, you *can* get there from here. If an audience member asks a question and you need to return to a previous visual, simply hit that slide number followed by the Enter key to take you there.

TIP 277: Keep Your Laser Pointer Under Control

Some presenters have a love-hate relationship with their laser pointers. While a pointer is far preferable for pinpointing a significant piece of data on the screen rather than a vague reference such as, "You'll notice there that . . . ," a pointer also can be annoying and troublesome.

Presenters find it difficult to remember to turn them off and on, to find them once they have laid them aside, and to control them with pinpoint accuracy. Presenters gesturing as they talk while the pointer is still on can send audience members dodging and darting. Pointers can damage the eyes of anyone inadvertently caught in the beam's path. If you really need them, control them. If you do not need them, find another gadget that's not so dangerous and annoying.

TIP 278: Switch Off Your Screen Saver Before You Begin

You may be embarrassed when your spouse's baby pictures or your favorite college slogan pops up in full view. Also, set your laptop so that it does not automatically go into sleep mode during your extended elaboration on a key point or during the question-and-answer period. Otherwise, you can return to your computer expecting to advance to the next slide and discover that it takes a very long time to wake up.

TIP 279: Always Have Backup Visuals in Case of Technical Problems

A removable disk, a CD, transparencies, slides, video, or handouts—any of these will fill the bill. However, it is naive to think that you will never need a backup.

TIP 280: Allow Extra Time for Equipment Setup

Gone are the days when you can just walk in and start talking. Even on good days when all that is supposed to be compatible really is, setup takes time. Unless you have sent a scout ahead to check things, allow yourself time to look for an extension cord, replace a projector bulb, find fresh batteries for the microphone, locate the missing clip for the lapel microphone, reboot the system and resize the images, lower or raise the screen, or move the projector stand so that the left side of the audience can see.

TIP 281: Make the Power Play

It is always a good idea to verify that your laptop has sufficient power to deliver your presentation at an acceptable speed. Lengthy video clips, complex graphics, and constant animation can hog power. Running through all your slides loads them into cache before the presentation, allowing them to load more quickly during your actual presentation.

TRANSPARENCIES

TIP 282: Consider the Pros and Cons Carefully Before Deciding to Use Transparencies

Pros

- Suitable for small or large audiences (up to 400 people)
- Easy to use and manipulate with very little practice
- Easy and quick to create
- Well-thought-out and professional appearance
- Easy to display only part of a transparency at a time (using a cover sheet)
- Easy to update and maintain
- Versatile with color, overlays, and drawings
- Transportable and easy-to-locate equipment (available almost anywhere)
- Reliable (equipment faults such as a burned out bulb can be corrected with little downtime)

Cons

- Considered an outdated presentation method by some
- Noisy when using older equipment
- Poor reproduction of photos and some graphics

TIP 283: Reveal a Line at a Time If You Intend to Elaborate Point by Point

Create suspense. Otherwise, the full text steals your thunder. Your elaboration becomes anticlimactic, and you seem to be belaboring the points that your audience has already skimmed in the first few seconds.

TIP 284: Frame Transparencies for Notes and for Easy Handling

You can jot notes on the frames, number the transparencies for easy reference, and return them to the proper order after use. Flip-Frames (plastic protective sleeves) made by 3M also have the added advantages of protecting your visuals from smudging and have holes in the left side that allow you to place them in a three-ring binder for easy storage and transport. The only drawback with frames—either plastic or cardboard—is the added bulk and weight.

TIP 285: Don't Leave a Glaring Light Between Transparencies

The glaring light distracts the audience when nothing is displayed on the screen. Either switch transparencies smoothly so that no light shows during the transfer or turn the projector light off as you make the switch. Another option is to cover the light bulb with a piece of cardboard. Then, before positioning the first transparency and while switching transparencies, flip the cardboard over the light to darken the screen.

TIP 286: Place a Blank Transparency Over a Printed One to Add Highlighting or Extra Text

This technique is useful when you want to ask for input from the audience and add to your visual spontaneously during your talk. When you finish your explanation or additional jottings on the overlay, you can remove the overlay without having altered the original.

TIP 287: Stand Next to the Screen Rather Than the Projector When Possible

Your standing by the projector often blocks the audience's view—particularly those seated near the front. Stand near the projector base only when you need to change transparencies frequently or when you need to write on the transparency as you speak.

TIP 288: Use a Pointer When Pointing to a Transparency on the Projector Base

Where should you point—to the projector base or to the screen? Let your stature be your guide. If you are six foot six, bending over to point to the projector base looks quite awkward. However, if you are five foot two, stretching to reach a screen looks equally awkward. And a pointer may or may not be available. Overhead projectors were invented for this very purpose—to allow a presenter to use or write on a transparency while still facing the audience.

Pointing with a shaking finger makes you look nervous. At best, it is a distraction because some will focus on your grooming (nail length and shape), and some will not be able to tell exactly where you are pointing. For a crisp pointer, use a pen or a swizzle stick.

TIP 289: Resist Packing Up While Making Your Closing Comments

Wait until you're completely finished with your presentation to file and put away your transparencies. Otherwise, you are signaling your audience that you have already tuned out and so should they.

FLIPCHARTS OR WHITEBOARDS

TIP 290: Consider the Pros and Cons Carefully Before Deciding to Use Flipcharts or Whiteboards

Pros

- Easy to move around the room and close to your audience
- Inexpensive
- Easy to create
- Informal, fresh, and spontaneous
- Readily available at most sites
- Easy to modify or customize on the spot
- Easy to update from presentation to presentation

- Easy to record interactions with a small group
- Easy to combine with more high-tech visuals in the same presentation

Cons

- Difficult for large audiences to see
- Time-consuming to prepare if using fancy lettering and art
- Cumbersome to transport and easily worn with use
- Lacks pizzazz—speaker's delivery style must carry the message
- Nonpermanent (erased information lost forever)

TIP 291: Write, Then Talk or Talk, Then Write

Writing and talking simultaneously may cause you to misspell, transpose, or omit words.

TIP 292: Pencil Notes to Yourself in the Margins

They will be visible to you but not to the audience.

TIP 293: "Code" Your Flipchart

First, make sure that your pad has enough paper for the entire presentation. Then leave one or two blank pages after each visual. This prevents the words on the following page from showing through when you're discussing the top page. Number or "code" pages in some way: Either turn up the corner of key pages that you will be referencing again and again or loop a piece of masking tape on the left side of the page and write in ink a title to the page so that you can catch the tape (as if it were a tab in a binder) and flip to the page easily.

Use colors consistently on preprinted charts so that your audience quickly differentiates main points from subpoints or key concept from illustration. For example, create titles in one color, key text in a second color, drawings in a third color, and accent marks such as bullet points in a fourth color.

TIP 294: Use a Broad-Tip Marker

The printing will be bolder. The thin markers that are great for writing on transparencies make lousy flipcharts.

TIP 295: Use Faintly Lined (Graph) Paper to Ensure
Printing Symmetry

If you do not want people doing a personality profile because your lines go
up into the wild blue yonder or descend to the depths, stay with lined
paper. It worked in kindergarten; why change?

TIP 296: Position Yourself to the Side of the Chart or
Board While Writing

If you stand in front of the chart as you write, your voice flows away from the
audience, and you completely lose eye contact with them. With one hand,
grab hold of the top of the chart (from the side back), and then write with
the free hand. The "anchor hand" at the back top will prevent you from
turning too far away from your audience as you write.

TIP 297: Tear Off Completed Pages and Tape or Hang
Them on the Walls

Sometimes it is nice to leave a trail of the group's or your collective wisdom
in full view. If you need to refer to ideas, it is much easier if the pages have
been permanently taped or hung rather than having to locate them again
in a full chart.

TIP 298: Cover a Page or Walk Away from It When
You've Finished Discussing Its Content

As long as you stay near the writing, audience members may become confused that your elaboration still relates to the chart or board. Move on—
both physically and mentally.

TIP 299: Use Two Charts Simultaneously—One for
Key Points, the Other for Supporting Detail

The two-chart system also makes it easy to compare or contrast ideas during
an ongoing discussion without cluttering one titled list. If you want to add

elaboration under bullet point four on chart A, move to the second chart to doodle.

VIDEO

TIP 300: Consider the Pros and Cons Carefully Before Deciding to Use Video

Pros

- Accurate representation of the content
- Strong indication of forethought and preparation

Cons

- May be expensive to produce
- May be difficult and expensive to update
- May have compatibility issues
- May be slow to load and play on computer because of file size
- Requires large amount of disk space to store on a computer

TIP 301: Be Creative About Uses

Business presentations often incorporate video clips to show products and services in action, to present testimonials from satisfied customers, to include expert briefings without requiring the expert to travel with the presenter, to use chief executive officer (CEO) introductions of new policies or strategies, to give virtual tours of supplier facilities to clients and prospects, and to train employees to handle various situations. The list of uses is limited only by a presenter's creativity.

TIP 302: Consider Stock Video for Generic Uses

Check out these Web sites for footage, among the many others you'll find by searching on "video stock footage": *www.fourpalms.com, www.cinenet.com, www.footage.net, http://members.aol.com/stockvideo/main.html/,* and *www. videosource.com.*

TIP 303: Consider Using the Original Analog Video If the Digital Video Segment Is Longer Than a Minute

Toggling between computer and video sources on your electronic projector is easy and eliminates any problems caused by file size. It also gives you the added advantage of a full-screen image.

HANDOUTS, BROCHURES, DATA SHEETS, AND OTHER LEAVE-BEHINDS

TIP 304: Consider the Pros and Cons Carefully Before Selecting These as Your Visuals of Choice

Pros

- Timing of the presentation unaffected by length of these visuals
- Easy maintenance and updating
- Inexpensive production
- Interactive design (encourages audience participation)
- Easy note-taking method
- Enhanced recall because audience keeps reference material

Cons

- Difficult to transport large numbers of lengthy handouts (must be mailed to site ahead of time)
- Increased danger of unauthorized and illegal copying and use of your material

TIP 305: Use Brightly Colored Paper for Pizzazz, When Appropriate

On occasion, be as creative in producing handouts as in producing any other visual. You can color-code sets of handouts to let your audience know that certain handouts belong to certain segments of your presentation. Or consider using different colors for certain pages within the packet to make access easy.

TIP 306: Take the Mystery Out of Delayed Distribution

Tell the audience up front what's in the reference materials to be distributed later. Some audience members become very irritated when they make the effort to take extensive notes on your presentation only to later discover that you will be making all the information available to them in a handout at the conclusion of your presentation. Instead, let them know your plans at the beginning. Note taking can then be their choice.

TIP 307: Create Documents for Later Reference

Build interest in handouts by letting the audience know that they contain information other than—not the same as—what you have already presented. Make the leave-behind additional information that would be too time-consuming to include in your oral presentation or that might be of varying interest to audience members.

TIP 308: Identify the Purpose to Determine When to Distribute Materials

Handouts may be intended for current interaction, for later reflection, for personal evaluation, or for on-the-job use. Distribute handouts *during* the presentation if they are designed to be interactive, with the audience listing, marking, noting, filling in the blanks, or otherwise reacting to your instructions. Distribute handouts *after* your presentation if they are simply reference material for later use. Do not encourage the audience to read along with you because they will read much faster than you talk, and you will lose eye contact and control.

TIP 309: Hold Visuals Toward the Audience While Referring to Specific Points

Although you may have called out a page number, an upward glance allows listeners a checkpoint to make sure that they are "with you" as you elaborate.

TIP 310: Make Documents Complete

Include any or all of the following on handouts: a summary of your key points, complex illustrations of key points, documentation and support from reference sources, a bibliography to encourage further reading and to give credit on ideas borrowed from others, articles from business or industry journals, and personal data on yourself. (The only exception to this principle of completeness is in situations where you have no intention of being complete—that is, where you are presenting information before a group of competitors such as during an association or industry meeting.)

TIP 311: Use the Notes Pages in the Slideshow as an
Option for Creating More Complete Handouts

As you create your slides, jot your elaboration in the notes section of that slide page—while you remember the exact verbiage you intend to use. You can change the preformatted bullets to sentences so that you have complete comments on all your key points.

If you're using PowerPoint, you'll do this on the Notes Page view. Then, once you have saved your presentation, go to File>Send To>Microsoft Word. This will take you to a pop-up menu that lets you select the handout layout. Select the top layout—Notes Next to Slides—and hit OK to copy your slides and notes to a Word document for your handout. You can even click the Paste Link radial button at the bottom of the pop-up window so that any changes you make to your slide presentation will be reflected automatically in the Word document handout.

The various popular presentation software packages will have different ways to accomplish this feat—preparing handouts as you prepare your slides.

Fast. Simple. Complete.

TIP 312: Remember That a Slide Generally Makes a
Lousy Handout, and a Handout Makes a Lousy Slide

Consider why this is true. By definition, a slide should be only the skeleton of an idea around which the presenter adds elaboration. A handout, on the other hand, should be complete and stand alone so that it makes sense when audience members leave the presentation and refer to it a month later.

Software designers may have confused an entire generation of presenters by calling one of the slide printout options the "Handout View." Many presenters have taken this easiest path in preparing a handout: Hit the Print button for a copy of their slides three or six to a page, and let listeners create their own notes to make a "handout" while listening.

The only problem with this philosophy? You have no control over what they understand and record—whether they get the point, miss the point, or don't care about the point. And letting your audience decide what you meant can be hazardous to their health and career—as well as to yours!

OBJECTS FOR DEMONSTRATION

TIP 313: Consider the Pros and Cons Carefully Before
Deciding to Do a Demonstration

Pros

- Provide realistic reinforcement of your words
- Increase audience participation with close observation

Cons

- Often difficult to transport
- Often expensive to replace when worn
- Often too small to enable the audience to see the most significant parts
- Often difficult for large audiences to see

TIP 314: Use Both the Object and a Blow-Up Diagram

They serve two different purposes and allow complete flexibility in referring to internal or external parts of the object in its entirety or to only a small detail.

TIP 315: Avoid Passing Around a Demo Object While You Are Talking

The object will compete with you for the group's attention.

TIP 316: Practice Thoroughly Any Required Assembly or Disassembly

Remember Murphy's law: Anything that can go wrong will go wrong. Make sure that you can make your point even if the demo does not work as you intend.

For further practice in learning what works visually and what does not, you may want to go to the industry publication *Presentations* magazine or *www.presentations.com*. The magazine reviews and rates the latest projection equipment. Even if you are not in the market to purchase a projector, remote control, or laser pointer, these reviews can educate you about available features to improve your presentations with visuals. Articles also give tips on visual "makeovers" much like makeup artists' before and after photos.

10

Q&A with Authority: Thinking on Your Feet Under Heat

Many a speaker exhausts his audience before he exhausts his subject. CAREY WILLIAMS

The difficulty of speeches is that you are perpetually poised between the cliché and the indiscretion. HAROLD MACMILLAN

A word too much always defeats its purpose. ARTHUR SCHOPENHAUER

But this is slavery, not to speak one's thoughts. EURIPIDES

Next to the invitation to speak, the customer's offhand comment, "Oh, by the way, leave a little time at the end for questions," causes the greatest concern among presenters. Why? There are numerous reasons.

Presenters may lack confidence in their understanding of the subject or project in general. They may dread not knowing the answer to a specific question. They may fear that someone will question their authority or the accuracy of their information. They may worry about stammering and faltering while delivering unplanned answers or being forced to answer questions they would rather did not surface before a group. They may be apprehensive about handling a hostile audience or participant. They may fear losing control of the audience and the presentation. They may feel that they have been put on the spot because of an unpopular answer. Any or all of these possibilities can cause high anxiety.

Why, then, do presenters even bother with question-and-answer periods? First of all, audiences have come to expect time for questions—it is their chance to get the presenter to meet the press, so to speak, particularly on controversial points.

In addition to meeting audience expectations and needs, Q&A periods benefit you, the presenter. First, questions let you apply your key points to the audience's specific situation. (This goal was accomplished in part by the audience analysis you conducted during the preparation phase; the Q&A period offers one last opportunity to make specific applications.)

Questions also provide feedback on how your message was received and give you a chance to clear up any misunderstandings. If you get a really off-the-wall question, you know that a key point was misinterpreted by at least one listener.

Another benefit is that Q&A periods build rapport with the group. Your answers show that you care about individual needs and understanding. Your taking the time to respond to questions indicates your goodwill and genuine interest in giving value to your audience. Q&A periods allow you to be less formal and more interactive than you may have been during the formal presentation; they are your chance to be spontaneous and witty. And nothing reveals your depth of knowledge, credibility, and communication skills as impressively as unrehearsed answers to unplanned questions.

Finally, Q&A sessions give you leeway in monitoring the length of the presentation. If you are running five or 10 minutes ahead of or behind schedule, you can get back on track during the time allotted for questions—a reassuring cushion, particularly during your first few presentations.

Let's get into the mechanics, then, of handling Q&A periods effectively.

CIRCLING THE TARGET: GENERAL GUIDELINES

TIP 317: Anticipate and Prepare for Questions

Audience analysis, the first step in preparing a presentation, always should include consideration of questions the group will have about your information and any opposing viewpoints. Plan for these questions specifically, and prepare succinct responses. You may choose to avoid a certain issue during your prepared remarks on the off chance that it will not surface during the Q&A period. But don't count on it. Be prepared with responses to, or at least acknowledgments of, opposing viewpoints.

TIP 318: Explain How and When You Will Take Questions

How long will you allow for questions? Will questioners have to come to the microphone, or can they be heard from their seats? Will listeners voice their questions or submit them on paper or by e-mail? Do you want to be interrupted during your prepared comments, or would you prefer all questions be held until the end?

Generally, it is best to announce that you will call for questions at the end of your presentation. Taking questions during your presentation may interrupt your train of thought, making it difficult to get back on track. Interrupting questions also may interfere with the audience's ability to digest the point you are making. Finally, with interrupting questions, you need to be creative in making smooth bridging statements from the answers back to your prepared comments. With "Now where was I?" as you return to your presentation outline, the questioner may feel the question was unwelcome and consequently may feel embarrassed or hostile toward you.

On certain occasions, you may decide to allow questions during your prepared comments—especially if they come from a boss, key decision maker, or other VIP whom you would not want to refuse an immediate answer. Sometimes, too, a presentation is so technical that questions delayed may be questions forgotten at a later point.

Either procedure—taking questions during or after the presentation—will work, provided you have given forethought to your chosen method.

TIP 319: Encourage Questions

Do not assume that if the group voices no questions, there aren't any. Audience members hold their tongues for any number of reasons. They may not have yet shifted gears to active participation. They may think that their questions are stupid and that they should have understood you the first time around. They may think that their questions would be of limited interest to others and do not want to monopolize the time for their own clarification. They may feel inept at wording the question succinctly. They may not want to risk others' hostility with a controversial viewpoint or question. Or they may have understood your presentation so thoroughly that they have no questions.

If you are typical of most speakers, you have three worries concerning audience questions. First, the audience doesn't understand your presentation well enough to ask questions. Second, they aren't interested in your subject. And third, they have decided they cannot trust anything you say. All of these spell trouble.

TIP 320: Use Open Body Language to Invite Questions

To encourage questions, make sure your body language shows openness to the audience—wide-open arms, upturned palms, alert posture, raised eyebrows, a smile, movement toward the audience. Body language either welcomes or discourages interaction.

TIP 321: Invite Questions with Appropriate Phrasing

The least effective solicitation is to mumble, "Are there any questions?" as you glance up briefly and then return to your notes, adding, "Fine. If there are no questions, I'll move along so that we can finish on time." By contrast, "What questions do you have?" lets a group know that you assume there will be questions and that you plan to answer them.

TIP 322: Use Humor to Demonstrate Your Openness

Participants are sometimes apprehensive to ask questions because they do not know how safe the environment is. For example, will their questions seem dumb or trivial to others? Will you be defensive or argumentative? Therefore, it may help to begin with humor simply to show your approachableness and goodwill toward the group.

For example, speaker Allen Klein sometimes asks, "Who wants to ask the first question?" If no one speaks up, he then says, "Okay, then who wants to ask the second question?"

Other comments that lend a light approach: "Surely, I didn't muddy the water so badly that nobody even has a question?" or "Somebody ask a question to let me know you at least understand the goal here in this campaign and have some interest—otherwise, just shoot me and put me out of my misery."

TIP 323: Give the Brave a Verbal Pat on the Back

Your affirmations following listeners' questions ("That's an excellent question," "Thanks for asking that," "I'm glad you brought that up because . . .") encourage others to risk asking their questions. Do take care, however, not to establish this as a routine pattern because after awhile the same comments begin to sound insincere. And when you are asked an obviously hostile question, such a comment can further exasperate the audience member.

TIP 324: Never Announce a Certain Amount of Time or a Specific Number of Questions

To do so limits your flexibility and creates dangers along the way. If you announce that you will take questions for half an hour and you get only two questions, the audience walks away with the impression that you gave a disappointing presentation that did not generate the expected interest.

If you say that you will take another three questions and the third question is a hostile one, you may be forced to end on a negative note from which it will be difficult to recover.

Stay flexible simply by making a general statement that you will take a few questions before you wrap up your presentation. Then, if there are none or only a few, you are safe to go directly into your prepared close. And if you get a challenging question or if a negative issue surfaces, you can prolong the discussion until you can find an opportunity to bridge to a more positive closing note.

TIP 325: Experiment with a Variety of Methods to Pose Questions

If you anticipate difficulty in generating questions, try distributing index cards at the beginning or end of the session, and ask participants to jot down their questions and pass them to the front. You or a colleague can sort through the cards, selecting the questions likely to benefit the most listeners. This technique gives you maximum control and flexibility while still showing responsiveness to the audience.

You also can generate questions with a hand-raising opinion poll: "How many of you think it would be feasible to raise this amount of money in six months' time?" (Take a count.) "In a year?" (Take another count.) "Caroline, you raised your hand for six months. What prompted that opinion?" Such informal probing relaxes the group, encourages openness, and establishes a comfortable climate for expressing viewpoints.

You also can pose your own questions. For example: "A question groups frequently ask me and that may be of interest to you is. . . ." Or "A question Bill Maxwell raised at our last meeting may still warrant discussion. He wanted to know if. . . ." Or "An issue I didn't get into during my earlier remarks is. . . . Do any of you have a particular concern about how . . . ?"

You may also want to repeat questions or comments overheard prior to the presentation or during breaks. For example: "Before the session, I heard someone express the idea that. . . . How many of you agree?" This follow-up on your part gives audiences time to consider their own ideas and questions and shows that you take their issues seriously.

TIP 326: Decide Whether to Repeat or Not to Repeat the Question

If the sound in the room is so poor that an audience member's question cannot be heard, you certainly should repeat it for all to hear. In some instances, if appropriate, you may want to repeat the question simply to give yourself time to think.

However, do not repeat a question in a small-group setting, where everyone obviously heard it the first time. Doing so is redundant and makes you sound like a parrot.

Never repeat hostile questions because it is difficult to do so without sounding hostile or defensive yourself. Another danger is that you reinforce the negative thought or opposing viewpoint in your audience's mind.

TIP 327: Set Boundaries During the Q&A

Set boundaries at the beginning of the session concerning the kinds of questions you will take, the number of questions you will have time for, and those best suited to respond to each. For example: "For security reasons, I'll ask you not to bring up the issues of X and Y." Or "We won't let ourselves get into Z because of the current litigation." Or "I prefer to deal with questions in the areas of A and B rather than C, which headquarters has requested be addressed to them by e-mail."

Comments such as these issued at the beginning set the stage for your control of what follows.

If someone asks an irrelevant question, respond that you will address it during a private dialogue at the break; in this way, you avoid wasting the group's time but still seem responsive to the listener's needs. This practice is also effective for handling questions unrelated to your expertise or experience.

TIP 328: Remember That You Do Not Have to Answer Every Question

If you consider a particular question out of line, too personal or confidential, irrelevant, or of little interest to the rest of the group, you can deflect it, reroute it, challenge it, or simply defer to an expert. "I'm afraid that's outside my area of expertise; would someone else like to respond?" "Jason, I'm curious about why you're asking that question; didn't you and Casey work those issues out earlier?" "I understand why you're asking that question, but I think it would be more advantageous to focus on. . . ."

Select the questions you want to answer. Reframe them the way you want to answer them. Bridge back to your key points.

TIP 329: Don't Let a Few Overzealous Participants Monopolize

As the presenter, you have responsibility to see that all audience members have full access to pose questions and that no one controls the show and "shuts down"—or creates an atmosphere that discourages—others. Even a remark about a pressing deadline or redundancy can discourage the more timid participants.

Tactful wording is typically your best tool: "Juanita, can you hold that next question? Let's take one from Omar first." Or "I regret that we do not have time for any more of your questions and comments—which, by the way, I found very perceptive and insightful. But we do need to wrap this session up. I'll be around for a few more minutes and then back in my office all afternoon if anybody wants to follow up one on one."

TIP 330: Listen to the Question

This is not always as easy as it sounds. If you are nervous, if you are silently scolding yourself about a previous error, if you are worrying about the time, or if you are confronted by a listener's hostile body language, it is easy to miss the point of what someone is asking. Such distractions can make you fumble a question you could have fielded easily otherwise.

Another difficulty here is that the asker may provide too much background or irrelevant information before getting to the point. And sometimes even the asker does not have a clear understanding of what his or her question is!

To avoid giving an off-base answer, clarify cloudy questions by probing: "Let me make sure I understand you correctly. You want to know if . . . ?" Or "Is your question whether . . . ?" Or "Are you asking if it's possible to . . . ?"

Do your best to understand the question being asked before concentrating on your rebuttal to the asker's viewpoint. Finally, show that you are listening by your attentive body language, such as leaning forward, tilting your head in reflection, and maintaining steady eye contact.

TIP 331: Pause to Think Before You Answer

Even if your response comes quickly to mind, pause before rushing ahead with it. With frequently asked questions in particular, it is tempting to give a canned answer. With a little forethought, however, you can customize your answer, making it even more responsive to the asker.

To buy additional thinking time, remove or put on your eyeglasses, take a sip of water, stride to another spot in the room before turning to face the group, or tilt your head and rub your chin, as if reflecting on the question.

You also can buy thinking time by commenting on the question itself: "Hmmm. That's a tough one." "That's a very perceptive question." "I anticipated someone asking that, and I don't know if you'll agree with my answer, but. . . ."

By responding, "I need to think about that one a moment," and then repeating the question aloud—"Let's see, what would I recommend if . . . ?"—you interject a pause that renews attention and curiosity about the serious reflection required.

And of course, you may opt not to answer at all: "I'm not at liberty to answer that now." "That piece of the puzzle is still in the works." "Please let me get back to you on that later."

TIP 332: Direct Your Answers to the Entire Audience

Maintain eye contact with the asker as you begin your response, and then, after a few seconds, glance away and sweep the entire group. If necessary, start specific and then make your comments generic enough for the entire group's interests.

Remember, you are not obligated to satisfy every questioner completely; some will insist on asking several follow-up questions. Others may persist in presenting their viewpoints even after you have given your answer. To prevent being locked into a dialogue with one member of your audience, answer briefly, break eye contact with the asker, and then turn to the entire group and ask for the next question.

TIP 333: Answer to Reinforce Your Points

Responses such as, "I'm glad you brought up that issue because it gives me a chance to elaborate on . . . ," are a way to align listeners' questions with points you really want to emphasize. You also can respond in a way that broadens or narrows the scope of a question's focus. "The issue that most of the industry will be concerned with is *X;* therefore, let me answer in this broader context." Or "Yes, that's the big-picture problem, but let me bring it a little closer to home with the more specific issue of *Y.*"

So go in either direction to reinforce your viewpoint or message.

TIP 334: Think on Your Feet with the SEER Format®

This acronym can help you formulate strong, spur-of-the-moment answers:

S = Summary (one-sentence statement of your answer)

E = Elaboration (key points to support your answer)

E = Example (specific illustration that will clarify and make the key points memorable)

R = Restatement (restatement of summary)

Here are two examples of this acronym in use:

Question: "Do you think leasing more space in this building will solve our overcrowded conditions permanently?"

Answer:

S: "No, I don't see leasing more space here as a permanent solution."

E: "The available space is not suitable for the kinds of shelving we want to install. For another thing, the extra space doesn't open to the outside corridor. Therefore, the traffic to the registration desk will still create peak-hour waiting lines. Neither will the extra space accommodate the additional 200 or so visitors expected during the spring."

E: "If you'll remember we tried—unsuccessfully—to alter the traffic pattern two years ago by leasing more space on the first floor. People just wouldn't walk to the end of the hall to take the alternate route. Remember Frank Tanner's comment about his people not even having time to reach the coffee machine in 15 minutes, much less take a break once they got there?"

>R: "So, no, I don't consider leasing more space in this building a permanent solution to the overcrowded conditions."

Question: "Does your company really care about the 'small customer'?"

Answer:

>S: "Yes, we most definitely care about 'small customers.' They keep us in business."

>E: "In fact, 70 percent of our volume comes from accounts we've labeled small businesses. We'd rather have 100 customers doing $50 to $75 a month with us than one customer doing half a million dollars a month. That's our philosophy. We think we get a broader perspective on the industry dealing with a variety of small businesses. We even print a catalog just for small businesses, showing products and services geared toward their specific needs. They also have their own 800 number for telephone support."

>E: "Just last week an operations VP for one of our accounts told me that because we'd learned so much about the account's business by selling to them, they've decided to use us on a consulting contract basis instead of hiring a permanent purchasing agent. We'll place their orders for related products supplied by their vendors. It's a real partnership. We'd like to do that with all our customers."

>R: "So, yes, we do care about the small customer."

This format should make it much easier for you to be a SEER and to think on your feet. It gives you a structure for responding in a concise way to ensure maximum impact and recall.

TIP 335: Defer Questions to Others with Special Expertise

This practice will win the support of the person you deferred the question to and respect from the audience for your self-confidence and honesty.

TIP 336: Take Care Not to Respond with More Than They Want to Know

Maybe most important of all: When you field a question, be brief. If you take 10 minutes to answer the first few questions, some participants may fear antagonizing less interested audience members by asking one that could lengthen your presentation by another half hour.

TIP 337: If You Do Not Know, Say So

Nothing makes people believe what you *do* know like admitting what you do *not* know. Never be afraid to say simply, "I don't know. I'll have to check on that and get back to you." And then do so.

TIP 338: Conclude the Q&A Period with a Summary

It is a good idea to prepare two closings: one that ends your prepared comments and leads into the Q&A period and one that wraps up the entire presentation.

If you are lucky, you may get a final question that is a great lead-in to your prepared closing. If so, use it as a smooth segue to your summary. But don't count on it.

In any case, never let your presentation limp to a close by following the last question with, "Well, if there are no more questions, that's about all, folks." Instead, firmly conclude with your prepared remarks—that pithy quote, rhetorical question, clever anecdote, or summary that will challenge your audience to action.

TACKLING THE TEN TOUGH TYPES

The Hypothetical Question

Be careful not to get trapped here. Often when people ask a hypothetical question, they have an agenda—they are looking for a forum to express their own opinion. Whatever answer you give will be "wrong," and they will change the details about their hypothetical situation and proceed to set you straight about what will or will not work. When this is the case, express any disagreement with assumptions, and say so if you think a particular hypothetical situation is highly unlikely.

Do, however, distinguish between a hypothetical situation and an example posed for clarification purposes. Generally, the difference is the intention or motive behind the question.

TIP 339: Sidestep the Details of the
Hypothetical Situation

Refocus by responding, "We have so many real-life situations needing our attention that I'd rather stick to the concrete facts if you don't mind." Or

"There are so many unknowns and variables in hypothetical cases that it's difficult to give a meaningful response to that situation." Or "I prefer to stay focused on the current mission in formulating policy for our charitable contributions. For the present situation, I still consider. . . ." Or "In the case of [topic], are you asking . . . ?"

TIP 340: Probe for the Real Issue and Address That Concern

By all means, address any real concerns behind hypothetical questions posed: "Is your concern in raising that question the safety issue?" If the audience member confirms that the safety issue is what prompted the hypothetical situation, then you can proceed to comment in general on the safety issue rather than getting bogged down in hypothetical details.

The Two-Option Question

With this question, the asker tries to pin you down to a forced response in which he or she designs the limited answers: "Can we refurbish the equipment for less than $100,000?" "Do you think Jan can handle the job successfully?" "Which do you think is the better supplier for this project—vendor A or vendor B?" The problem in responding is being trapped into giving an "absolute" answer with which you are uncomfortable.

TIP 341: Choose an Option Only If You're Comfortable in Doing So

If you can answer a question with a simple yes or no, choice A or choice B, do so. If you do not see the issue as a black-or-white situation, explain why: "We have to be careful not to back ourselves into a corner with either course of action. We shouldn't forget the extenuating circumstances that might alter the picture." Or "I don't think a simple 'yes' or 'no' does justice to the issue." Or "We'd make a mistake to state this in either-or terms. There are so many variables at play here, such as X, Y, and Z." Or "Neither of those choices sounds workable to me. I don't think we're asking the right question."

TIP 342: Expand Your Options If Neither of the Posed Options Suits You

You can expand the options with a reply like, "I think we have more than those two alternatives. Rather than choice A or choice B, a third possibility is to. . . ." Or "I'd suggest we not limit our thinking at this early stage in the project." Or "I'm not satisfied to make a decision at this point. Although I don't see other alternatives at this point, I'm sure we can think creatively and come up with a different solution before we're forced to make a decision on this matter."

The Long-Winded Question

Generally, there are two reasons for long-winded questions: (1) inarticulate people who think as they ramble and (2) articulate people who like to show off their thinking and speaking. The former appreciate help and need a guide. The latter appreciate a forum, and need a muzzle.

TIP 343: Help the Inarticulate Word the Question

Listen long enough until you are sure you understand the question, and then help the asker phrase the question: "So do I understand your central question to be . . . ?" Or "Excuse me, but I think I have the drift of your question. Let me respond by saying that. . . ." The inarticulate rambler generally will appreciate the help and nod approvingly when you take the proverbial ball and run with it.

TIP 344: Use Your Body Language to Help the Questioner "Wind Down"

Nod that you understand the question, walk toward the asker as if accepting the question and start to back away, or break eye contact and glance back at

Help long-winded, rambling questioners.

the entire group as if ready to respond when given an opening. All this body language tends to signal the asker that time is growing short.

TIP 345: Interrupt with a Short-Answer Question

To interrupt by talking over someone with a statement is considered rude. However, to interrupt with a question is less obviously an intrusion. In fact, a question can be a sign of interest. Listen long enough to grasp what the person is saying, and then ask a question about something he or she has just said that can be answered with just a word or two. When the talker stops the ramble and train of thought to answer your question, you, the presenter, have the floor back.

Unintelligible Question

Sometimes you're unable to understand a question because the asker has a heavy dialect or is fuzzy in his or her phrasing.

TIP 346: Pick One Phrase or Part of the Question and Use It to Frame a New Question

Asking someone more than twice to repeat the question often causes frustration and embarrassment, yet you cannot answer a question you cannot understand. If a heavy accent, misused words, or improper syntax has rendered a question unintelligible to you, most likely others in the audience will have the same difficulty. So when you do your best to guess at what the person is asking and frame a new question to answer, most in the audience will admire your courtesy in not embarrassing the questioner with a repeated barrage of "Ask it again."

TIP 347: Ask Someone Seated Nearby for Help

Sometimes others in the audience can understand the accent or make sense of the syntax and repeat the question for you. For example: "I'm sorry I'm having difficulty hearing—would someone help me?"

TIP 348: Assume Responsibility for the Clarity Issue Yourself

Try never to embarrass the asker. Phrasing and intonation can be extremely important in your response: "*I'm* having difficulty . . ." versus "I can't make out what *you're* saying." The latter statement may come across as if you are blaming the other person.

If you are witty, you may try a humorous approach at your own expense. For example: "I'm sorry, but I'm having a senior moment. I'm missing the point—would somebody translate for me?" Or "I missed my caffeine this morning—somebody's going to have to say it much slower and louder for me. And dumb it down a couple of grade levels, will you?" Or "They've had me locked up in MIS far too long—you're going to have to write that question out and e-mail it to me so that I can translate it into the gobbledygook that I typically hear."

Such humorous remarks make you appear gracious to the audience and relieve the tension of the moment.

The Off-the-Record Question

Even in a corporate or other nonmedia setting, you may be asked questions "off the record," meaning that the participant or group will consider your response your personal opinion rather than the "official" word. Typically, you receive most of these questions in one-on-one conversations at breaks during your presentation or before or after the meeting.

TIP 349: Put It on the Record

When asked an off-the-record question, take care to respond to a bigger audience than one or two. For example, if during a meeting break someone asks for your opinion about whether a recent merger will really result in layoffs, despite the fact that management has officially announced that it would not, you might respond this way: "Probably that issue is on the minds of several people in the group. Why don't I address that when we reconvene." Then do so. Whatever comments you make before the entire group will be much harder to take out of context and misconstrue than had you expressed them privately and "unofficially" to an individual.

TIP 350: Don't Say Anything That You Don't Want on the Record

It's far too easy for your words to be taken out of context or to be misquoted. Ask any author, movie star, sports figure, or politician. Understand that very few things are "off the record," and respond as if your comments would be published in the corporate newsletter, city newspaper, or industry or business journal tomorrow morning.

The "Dumb" Question

Do not chance cutting off someone who is asking what sounds like a dumb question that may turn out to be an intelligent one after all. Sometimes "dumb" questions are the result of advanced, complex thinking that has not yet occurred to you. Such a question may be relevant, but you do not understand the connection because of limited expertise in the subject.

TIP 351: Probe to Clarify Any Connections

Take care not to communicate with your body language that the asker is "off base." Assume that the question has merit until you know otherwise. Probe prudently: "I'm afraid I'm not following you. Would you explain further exactly how X relates to Y?" Or "I'm confused. Help me understand the connection between cost of X and the feasibility of Y?"

TIP 352: Decide Whether It Is On or Off the Subject and Respond Accordingly

If, after probing, you determine the question to be on the topic at hand, you can respond with no one being put on the spot. If the question is truly out in left field, you can treat it as an "off the subject" question and offer to discuss it one on one with the asker after your presentation.

The Show-Off Question

Generally, this "question" is a monologue—either an opinion on an issue or a barrage of data and facts. Then, after the dump, the asker tacks on a limp question at the end, such as "Wouldn't you agree?" or "Don't you think that's true?" or "Have you considered all this before making your recommendation?"

TIP 353: Ask for a Restatement of the Question

If this kind of questioner persists, you may have to add a comment such as the following to keep him or her from monopolizing the situation: "I'm not sure I understand the question in all this. Would you please restate your question?" or "Were you just stating an observation, or is that a question?" After some fumbling, the participant may or may not come up with a question that you can answer briefly and use to regain control.

TIP 354: Acknowledge the "Comment" and Then Ask for the Next Person's Question

When you recognize such a "question," comment briefly, break eye contact, and move on to the next question. Examples: "Thank you for that observation." "Good information to have." "You have a point." "That's one way to look at the issue." "You sound as though you've had some experience with similar situations." "I'm sure others may feel as you do." "That's something else we may want to consider in the decision."

The Limited-Interest Question

The answer to such questions holds great interest for the asker and has little or no value for others in the audience. Taking time to give answers of even two to three minutes can lose an audience; others take such occasions to leave and make a phone call, check their e-mail, or get a cup of coffee. For this reason, answering such questions presents a risk.

However, the bigger risk in giving more than a 15-second answer is that others will assume that you do not understand your audience well, that you assume that others share the interests, needs, and situation of the asker, or that you do not know how to control the discussion.

TIP 355: Bridge from the Limited Perspective to the Larger Issue at Hand

Examples: "With reference to your specific situation, my opinion is that. . . . But the larger issue here seems to be. . . ." Continue by expanding the idea to apply to the entire audience.

TIP 356: Defer to a One-on-One Discussion Later

Or ask: "Does anyone else have that concern?" Pause and look around; if no one responds, continue: "Well, let me address that briefly; then let's talk about that later, one on one." Then break eye contact and move on.

Multiple Questions

Have you ever seen reporters in a feeding frenzy with a politician trapped in a scandal? Or how about moderators feeding write-in questions to technical experts on an industry panel? In attempting to respond to long, complex questions with irrelevant information thrown into the pot, you may have trouble remembering everything that was asked along the way. When this is the case, you have several choices:

TIP 357: Answer the Questions You Remember

People forgive short memories. They do not forgive wrong or unpopular answers.

TIP 358: Answer Only the Last Question

Ditto the preceding paragraph. By the time you finish a lengthy last answer, many people will forget that you never answered other questions leading up to the last one. Or they will consider the last question as the predominant, culminating one that the asker intended for you to focus on with your response.

TIP 359: Answer Only the Most Important Question

You can always refer to a ticking clock and say that in the interest of time, you would like to "boil things down" to the most relevant, important question of them all. Then respond at length to that one question or issue.

TIP 360: Select Only the Questions You Like

In the school system, professors get to choose the questions; students have to supply the answers. After graduation day, however, the tables are turned. For the most part, you do not have to answer the questions that you are asked. You can defer some of them with a response like, "If I understand completely, you've asked me four good questions. Let me answer the first two and come back to the others later if there's time." Or "Those last two questions really fall outside my area of expertise, but I'd be happy to address the first matter you raised."

TIP 361: Ask the Questioner to Repeat the Questions One at a Time

Responding to questions is not a memory test. You can write them down or delegate remembering them to your asker: "You've asked five relevant questions. I'd like to respond to all of them. Please repeat them one at a time, and let's take them in order." After you have responded to the first one, ask for the second and so forth.

The Hostile Question

People ask hostile questions for any number of reasons: (1) They disagree with what you have said or have wrong information. (2) You have not established credibility with them. (3) They have misunderstood you. (4) They think they are "saving the day" for their organization. (5) Their personality makes them always look for the cloud in every silver lining. (6) They have a hostile tone and facial expression without realizing it. (7) They are angry with someone else and are taking it out on you—consciously or unconsciously. (8) Their question is neutral, but you have had a bad day and are "reading hostility into the question."

TIP 362: Rephrase a Legitimate Question Minus the Hostile Tone

If the question is "Why are you demanding six years of experience for all subcontracted work? I think that's totally unreasonable," try rephrasing it to emphasize its validity, and then respond: "Why do we think six years' experience is necessary? Well, first of all. . . ."

Don't feel that you have to refute an opposing view in great detail, particularly if the hostile view is not well supported itself. Simply comment: "No, I don't think that's the case." No elaboration is necessary. Your answer will sound authoritative and final and will make the asker appear rude and argumentative if he or she rephrases and continues.

Rephrase a legitimate question, minus the hostile tone.

Above all, avoid matching hostility with hostility; try to maintain a congenial tone and body language. The audience almost always will side (or at least respect and empathize) with the person who remains calm and courteous.

Keep in mind that *how* you answer questions will be remembered more clearly and for much longer than your words.

TIP 363: Acknowledge and Accept Feelings

Try to determine possible reasons for any hostility. By acknowledging and legitimizing the feelings of the asker, you may defuse the hostility and help him or her receive your answer in a more open manner. Examples: "It sounds as though you've been through some difficult delays with this supplier," or "I don't blame you for feeling as you do, given the situation you describe. I'm just glad that has been the exception rather than the rule in working with this audit group."

TIP 364: Understand That Hostility May Be a Personality Pattern

In some cases, the questioner's hostility may be a reflection of his or her business agenda or personality and have little to do with you. Simply let the asker vent emotions, then briefly state your opinion and move directly on to the next question.

Some questioners use a pseudocourteous tone to wrap a hostile question. If so, reply with genuine courtesy—skip the sarcasm.

TIP 365: Agree with Something the Questioner Has Stated

If possible, try to find something within the hostile questioner's comment and question with which you can agree. This typically diffuses some of the hostility and the inclination to argue with whatever response you provide. Then give your answer.

TIP 366: Try Humor at Your Own Expense

Example: Throw your hand across your heart as if you've been shot and say, "You really got me with that one." Other options: (looking around the group and toward the back of the group) "Where are friends when you need them?" or (said with a twinkle in your eye and a smile) "I can see I've really impressed you with my skill, expertise, and track record on this topic," or "I was thinking of shutting down this discussion a little early. Maybe now's a good time." Pretend for a moment to do so, before proceeding to answer as calmly as possible.

TIP 367: Relay the Question

You can relay it to another person or back to the asker: "Su Lin, do you want to try to answer that question?" "I feel uncomfortable responding to that question, Jacob. Maybe you'd like to tell us how you'd answer if you were in my place."

If you think the hostility is limited to one person's viewpoint, get the group to respond on your behalf by asking a question like "Do any of the rest of you agree with that viewpoint?" or "Does anyone else want to respond?" The silence will speak volumes to the asker.

Maybe the very idea of asking questions got a bad rap when, as children, we were told never to question parental decisions or commands. Schools, too, sometimes reinforce the idea that questions negatively challenge an instructor's authority. Certainly, we all remember the class smart aleck, whose every question was a challenge. Or maybe we have seen too many TV courtroom dramas, where the judge instructs the witness in a booming voice, "Just answer the question."

Don't let such memories and experiences keep you from making your presentations all they can be. Allow plenty of time for questions, and watch your audience members' mood, interest, and body language shift from low gear into high. Questions can help you clarify, tailor, and reinforce your key points. Not least of all, Q&A periods are your best forum for expressing openness, genuineness, courtesy, and goodwill toward your audience.

11

Interactivity as Part of Your Style: Stir, Simmer, Sizzle, Snap, and Stifle

There is no cure for insomnia like listening to yourself talk.   UNKNOWN

After-dinner speeches can make you feel dumb at one end and numb at the other end.
                                                  UNKNOWN

Amateurs and egotists usually share one fault in common when making a talk. They try to impress rather than express.   UNKNOWN

The best time to end your speech is when you feel the listening is lessening.   UNKNOWN

People interact with their computers, DVDs, TVs, cell phones, home security systems, ATMs, and airline check-in systems. Team members give 360-degree feedback to their peers and supervisors. They send suggestions to the senior executives by e-mail. Suppliers survey clients to ask, "How are we doing?"

So when it comes to presentations, audiences assume that you will build in a two-way dialogue and interactivity—that you will not simply provide an information dump and walk away, thinking you have communicated and achieved your objective.

Not only do today's audiences demand interactivity, but also you as presenter will find that it serves some useful purposes of your own: Interactivity helps cement key points. It provides a change of pace and gives audiences a chance to "catch their breath" almost as much as a physical break. Interactivity can add levity to the atmosphere and also help you to build rapport. And depending on which techniques you choose, interactivity can "break the ice" among audience members and encourage them to get to know each other.

Neither do audience-involvement techniques necessarily need to be time-consuming or complex. In fact, some audience-involvement techniques do not even require your audience to speak at all. For example, just calling an audience member's name grabs their attention and says to the rest of the group: "I'm aware of you as individuals, with specific needs, issues, and concerns."

Creativity is your only limitation.

INTERACTIVITY TO SUIT YOUR STYLE

TIP 368: Ask the Audience to Guess at Statistics Before Revealing Them

Chart after chart of data can be deadly. For variety, create an opportunity to make your information "stick" with your listeners. For example, instead of telling them what the accuracy rate was on filling orders last quarter, have them guess the percent. Then reveal the actual statistic. Instead of telling them how successful the marketing campaign in the second quarter was, ask them to guess how many leads it generated as compared with other typical campaigns. Then ask them to guess the spike in sales during the first 30 days after the marketing campaign. Then reveal the numbers.

The best guessers likely will get a kick out of patting themselves on the back. And the poor guessers will be truly surprised. In both cases, the numbers will make much greater impact than had you simply reported them.

TIP 369: Tell a "Hero Story" Involving an Audience Member

Audiences like to participate vicariously as you recognize one of their own: "It seems that every division has one person who stands out as a mentor. Joan Gandee is her division's mentor" tends to make the group glance at Joan and think for themselves about their own mentors while you tell Joan's story.

You can discover such anecdotes as you research your audience. For example, if you are talking about the need to improve customer service in your organization, as you investigate, you undoubtedly will hear a few stories about those who provide exceptional service. Tell their stories in a specific situation as the model to strive for with all customers.

TIP 370: Ask an Audience Member to Share Examples or Experiences

A question such as "Can anyone give me an example of this principle of ethics at work in your community or organization?" customizes your point for a particular audience.

Make sure, however, that your group does have experiences to share. Otherwise, you are left with dead silence, making you look as though either you do not know your audience or they are bored with the topic. To prevent the dead silence, you can solicit volunteers ahead of time or simply make sure that you are aware of key people to call on specifically who are willing to provide examples or experiences.

Do be aware, however, of the danger of opening the floor to others: They may take longer than expected to tell their story. They may change the mood of your presentation. Or they may provide an example that contradicts your point.

TIP 371: Ask a Volunteer to Help You Demonstrate Something

Watch the energy level of the group rise. The entire audience engages in the action because they all will put themselves in the place of the one volunteer in front of the group with you.

TIP 372: Ask the Audience to Complete a Questionnaire or Worksheet

These do not have to be lengthy or complex. Provide a worksheet to determine their individual situation on the issue you will be addressing, such as the amount of insurance needed for a family of X with income of Y by two working parents. Or ask people to fill in the blanks as you give them a formula for computing how much they would need to save to pay for a child's college education 10 years down the road. Or ask them to calculate their sales closing ratio. After a two-minute pause, you may want to ask for responses so that you can comment on results, or you can use the interactivity only for individual reflection or motivation.

TIP 373: Survey the Audience

Surveys do not have to be scientifically valid to be intriguing or thought-provoking. You can conduct the survey orally on the spot. "How many of you have ever worked for an organization going through a merger? Let me see your hands" means that each listener has to tune in long enough for you to count affirmative responses. Audiences generally like to see how their opinions and experiences stack up against those of their peers.

Do not overuse this technique, however. Ask for a show of hands only when you intend to use the results in your next comment. Otherwise, this technique gets tiresome and seems senseless.

Or you can do written surveys. Ask an assistant to collect and sort responses at the beginning of the session so that you can report and comment on results later in your talk. Or you may want to survey your audience by e-mail days before your session to solicit facts, experiences, opinions, or questions to be addressed or used during your presentation. Both these survey methods engage people and tell them that you value their input.

TIP 374: Ask Volunteers to Transfer the Theoretical to the Practical

Do not leave new information or a motivational message in its raw form. That is, take it one step further by applying it to the job. Ask volunteers for real-world examples. How will the concept, policy, theory, procedure, or software package work back on the job next Wednesday? Call on someone to outline his or her understanding of the steps involved; then you can verify clarity and correct any misunderstandings.

TIP 375: Invite the Audience to Work Through a Process or Examine an Object

Such interactivity is particularly powerful in a sales presentation or in teaching a process or skill. Reinforcement through physical manipulation is not exactly a new concept.

I hear and forget
I see and I remember
I do and I understand
CONFUCIUS, 551–479 B.C.

TIP 376: Pause to Let the Audience Read Something to Themselves

The switch from listening to silent reading will be a welcome change of pace. A product data sheet. An eight-step marketing plan. A half-page status report. The two-paragraph summary from the audit report. A case study. There is no reason that you have to tell people simple, brief information they can read for themselves. Save your comments for the more complex job—the *interpretation* of what they have read. What do you want them to *do* about the information?

TIP 377: Ask the Audience to Brainstorm or List Something as Fast as Possible

Listing creates quick awareness in a more interactive way than lecturing. Brainstorming promotes creative thinking about possibilities—you may or may not want to lead the group to a conclusion about which of the ideas is best. If you have participants call out the ideas or items as one large group, you may or may not want someone to write them down so that you can refer to them later. If they make a list in small groups, you may ask all, a few, or only one team to call out their list at the conclusion of the activity. If one group reports their output, you can have other groups add only items or ideas *not* mentioned by the first.

TIP 378: Divide the Audience into Small Groups to Discuss an Issue

This interactivity works best with opinions—because almost everybody has one. The more controversial the issue, the better. Individuals have a brief opportunity to "vent" their feelings and opinions to someone—all simultaneously—and you do not necessarily have to listen. You can call on none, one, a few, or all groups to report quickly on their output or conclusions.

TIP 379: Ask a Rhetorical Question

Audience involvement does not always mean out loud. Rhetorical questions such as "What would you do if . . . ?" or "Has this ever happened to you?" engage an audience to think with you, even if they do not have to respond overtly.

TIP 380: Ask a Variety of Question Types to Achieve Different Purposes

> *Relay questions:* "That's a good question, Carlita. Thanks for bringing up that issue. Anybody have experience with that kind of situation?"
>
> *Direct questions:* "Michael, how would you respond to that issue if it came up in your department?"
>
> *Open questions:* "What are some of the changes you expect to see in the next six months?"
>
> *Closed questions:* "Do you expect any pushback from clients?"
>
> *The stir:* "The marketing group says that it is too expensive for the number of leads generated. The sales group loves the idea. The regional managers are undecided. So I'm bringing the idea directly to this committee. What are your thoughts on our chances for success with this campaign?"
>
> Always give careful consideration to how you phrase questions.

SUSTAINING THE MOMENTUM AND STAYING ON TRACK

TIP 381: Involve Your Audience Early to Establish the Pattern of Participation

> Audiences become set in their moods early. Signal your expectations clearly up front to create an atmosphere of "we're in this together" to make our time together beneficial. By instructing audience members to "Turn to the person on your left and give a 30-second description of your part in the project," you add variety and a personal touch to your overview.

TIP 382: Encourage Participation with Giveaways

> A chief executive officer (CEO) friend of mine carries a roll of one- and five-dollar bills with him, and the first time he tosses out a question and someone answers, he makes a big deal of handing them a dollar for responding. His "reward system" brings on a big laugh, sets a light tone, and encourages participation throughout the sessions with employees and suppliers because they never know who is going to get $1 or $5.
>
> For your purposes, you may give away organization trinkets such as coffee mugs, key chains, a sports jacket or two, a popular book, candy bars, or even

just a laminated poster of your key points. The giveaways aren't nearly as important as the fact that you are welcoming participation and humor.

TIP 383: Give Audiences Options and Control

With online shopping at midnight, unlisted phone numbers, pay-per-view movies, choose-your-own-ending novels, create-your-own greeting card lines, and e-learning courses delivered to the desktop, audience members—particularly those in training sessions—want to drive. They like to control what they learn, how they learn, in what order they learn, and to what depth they learn it. You as presenter have to be ready to accommodate them.

TIP 384: Provide Only a General Agenda

When you provide a specific topic outline, you limit your flexibility if you decide to alter your timetable to adjust to the interests of your group, to accept new issues raised by the group, or to accommodate other unexpected situations. Additionally, some people feel cheated that you did not cover certain points listed on the agenda. You often will receive comments and questions such as, "You skipped the part about X—what about that? It says here that you planned to cover that."

Instead, select one of these options: (1) List broad topic areas only, omitting all references to timing or (2) use a graphic design that omits any semblance of chronology but instead displays specifics in random order, size, and intensity.

TIP 385: Plan a "Start on Time" Buffer

Starting on time should be your standard. Otherwise, people will learn to ignore future announced times for your presentations. However, what do you do when the key decision makers are not yet in the room? Starting without them certainly means that you likely will have to repeat everything you have said—or chance that they will not go along with your recommendation because they did not hear foundational information.

As a work-around to such a dilemma, always plan a buffer: something to start "officially" for those who are present on time but something that you do not plan to use if all audience members are present at the beginning. For example, in a sales presentation with a client, this buffer might be asking and reconfirming a few details about the client's expectations for your presentation. In a training session, this buffer might be an icebreaker. In a management meeting, this buffer might be a recap of strategic goals that your presentation will address.

TIP 386: Place Items in Audience Members' Chairs to Start a "Mixer"

Ideas: A questionnaire or survey for which they have to get other people's input, a drawing for door prize to be given at the end of your talk, a brain-teaser that you will give the answer to later or reward the solver with a prize, a list of key issues you would like their ideas or opinions on, or brochures related to new products or services you will be presenting.

TIP 387: Use Music to Energize the Group

Retailers have learned that music makes shoppers move slower or faster. With slow music, they linger, browse, and buy more. With fast music, they buy impulsively and move on. Likewise, make mood music serve your presentation purpose.

Also consider background music before or after the presentation or during breaks. Music sets the mood and establishes a subtle connection between you and the audience. Your selection of music suggests your tastes and is bound to generate audience comments during the breaks—points of connection between you and the group.

TIP 388: Provide an Emotionally Safe Environment

Dominating audience members can quickly "shut down" timid ones. Impatient participants can rush talkers so that they feel inhibited about speaking up with an experience, example, or question. It is easy for presenters to focus on the body language and comments of the more vocal in the group and not notice that others have withdrawn. As the leader of a group interaction, a key task is equalizing the personalities to the degree that all feel comfortable to speak.

If things go wrong—if a long-winded person dominates, if someone feels embarrassed, if someone feels that he or she had no opportunity for input, if someone is bored—audience members will blame you. You are the host of your presentation.

TIP 389: Give People an Opportunity to Interact with Each Other as Well as with You

Providing a way for them to remember each other's names gets you off to a good start on this mission. You have several options: Provide name plates or tent cards for panelists or other presenters and all participants around the room. Or have audience members write their names informally on a piece of paper and construct their own informal tent card in front of them. Also, make name cards portable (affixed) so that they are visible on the person during breaks. Another alternative is to ask audience members to introduce themselves before speaking or asking a question.

For specific projects or interactions, divide the audience into groups of four to six people each. Seven is too many and three is too few for most activities. Groups involve everyone, create a sense of camaraderie and ownership, and provide a variety of viewpoints and opportunities for peer networking and coaching.

TIP 390: Use a Variety of Ways to Select Groups

They can all select a piece of candy and divide according to the leftover candy wrapper. Draw a color. Name an animal. Divide by color of eyes, hair color, first names starting with the letters *A* to *H,* state of birth, and so forth.

TIP 391: Make People Feel Smart, Not Stupid

This principle particularly holds true in training sessions. Help participants master concepts and grow in self-confidence as they move through the session rather than making them feel overwhelmed and deficient. Although they may leave admiring your knowledge, they will not likely move any closer to the learning objective.

In an informative presentation, rather than a game of "gotcha" while you reveal little-known data and decisions, it is typically better to lead your audience along with you toward conclusions by educating them as you go. That is, explain terms, criteria, processes, and reasoning. As they understand more about the subject, they likely will move closer to the goal.

TIP 392: Make People Feel Independent, Not Dependent

Show people not just the destination but the roadmap to get there. If they hear your presentation and agree with your conclusions and recommendations but then cannot explain them or justify them to anyone else, you have fallen short. If they are the only decision makers and they never have second thoughts about their signoff, the presentation may stand. However, should the listeners have to justify the decision to others or have a change of heart, your job will be much tougher the second time around. Make an informative presentation a "do-it-yourself" kit when it comes to reasoning.

TIP 393: Keep Discussions Relevant

You are responsible for reigning in ramblers. You walk a fine line between inviting interaction, adjusting the time, controlling key input from audience members who may disagree, and unraveling the entire coherence of the presentation. Your key measuring stick is relevancy.

TIP 394: Explain Why Discussions Are Necessary or Germane to the Mission

Occasionally, audience members consider discussions accidental—presentations that get out of control through interruptions either because the presenter is unskilled or unprepared and someone has had to ask a question or insert an explanation.

Therefore, it is a good idea to point out that you *invite* discussion—that it is not unplanned wandering or a time filler because you ran out of soap.

TIP 395: Provide Interactions That Involve All Learning Styles—Visual, Auditory, and Kinesthetic

Some people remember best with visual activities—things they can see, such as wall charts, demonstrations, handouts, or slides. Other audience members do best with things that involve what they hear—your oral presentation, small-group discussions, videos that illustrate a key point with a real-life situation or story. Still others remember best those sessions that involve kinesthetic interactions—things that they do, model, role-play. They need to involve the sense of touch and movement and will retain more from a game they create or play, a brain teaser they unscramble, a piece of art they create, or equipment they operate.

TIP 396: Avoid Telling People What to Do Without Providing an Explanation

If you have children, you know that their first reaction to a directive ("Go wash your hands.") is always, "Why?" The same holds true for adults. Ask them to complete a survey, do a worksheet, or list six benefits of X, and their first reaction will be, "Why? What's the point? Why should I use brainpower on this?" Therefore, if you want maximum participation, tell the group up front.

TIP 397: Provide an Example with Instructions

"A picture is worth a thousand words" became a cliché for good reason: We need examples—clear, succinct, step-by-step visuals. So when you ask an audience to do something, do not talk theoretically. Be specific. Provide a model.

TIP 398: Write the Directions

With oral directions, some will listen; others will not and then will ask, "Now what are we supposed to do?" Result: You will have to repeat everything twice, taking double the time you intended. To anticipate this common occurrence, write directions in short form on a handout or slide.

TIP 399: Make Participation Optional

Keep in mind that audience participation works best when everyone has a choice. Pressure to participate—even to raise a hand in response to a question—may intimidate or even irritate some. You can prevent most hesitancy by knowing your audience and always selecting appropriate interactivity to accomplish your purpose. Your enthusiastic participation encourages others. In short, be your own cheerleader, but do not ask the audience to do anything that makes them uncomfortable.

12

Site Preparation: The Right Room with the Right Toys

To be ready to make a speech and not be asked is even worse than being asked to speak when you are not ready.   JACK HERBERT

Almost nobody listens to a commencement address, except a few parents in the last effort to get something for their money.   UNKNOWN

Murphy's law applies to planning presentations, specifically to site preparation: If it can go wrong, it will. This is why ensuring a good presentation starts long before the audience arrives. The following scenarios will give you an idea of the range of disasters waiting to happen:

The client scheduled my presentation in its corporate headquarters—on a day when all official conference rooms were occupied. So, a corner of the company cafeteria became our "room." No, not exactly, the *corner*. Scrunched in the corner would have been far better—at least we would have been out of the line of traffic. No, our U-shaped tables were set up at about a 10 o'clock position in the center of a very large rectangular room. This was the only spot with an opening large enough for 25 people to be seated together. A 3-foot-diameter column extended floor to ceiling in almost the exact center of our space. A few people had to lean around the column to see the visuals; I had to play peek-a-boo from up front. Stir into the mix the sounds, smells, and sights while 2000 employees paraded

179

through to eat lunch at the surrounding tables between the hours of 11:00 and 2:00.

Then there was the time I spoke at the Dallas Convention Center, where the sponsor had selected a room that could comfortably accommodate about half the number of attendees in the session. The unlucky half of the audience endured the entire 90-minute session seated on the floor in the back of the room, in the aisles, behind display tables, at my feet, and underneath and behind the two large projector screens.

And there was the day of musical chairs: On arriving at a client's building early to set up, I discovered a meeting in progress scheduled to end at the same time in the same room mine was slated to begin. That gave me exactly 60 seconds to let the first group exit, unpack my catalog case, rearrange the AV setup, and distribute materials to my own arriving audience.

I could go on and on. The list of things that can go wrong is endless:

- The AV equipment cord will not reach the outlet.
- The extension cord has a three-pronged plug, and the outlets are two-prong.
- There's a short in the projector's on-off switch.
- The flipchart stand is too high for your reach.
- Your laptop will not "talk" to the projector.
- The flipchart pad has only two pages left.
- The screen is lopsided, so your visuals look as though someone produced them lying down.
- There is no table to display your materials or notes.
- Carpenters are next door tearing out a wall.
- Hecklers are protesting in the hallway, harassing your attendees.
- The restrooms are a brisk 20-minute walk away.
- The room seats 500, and you are expecting 15.
- The room seats 15, and you are expecting 500.
- The carpet smells like insecticide, and someone in the front row is wheezing.
- The ceiling-mounted lighting flickers, causing eyestrain and migraines.

By the way, in the situations mentioned earlier, I *had* described to the client coordinator in charge of the cafeteria fiasco that people needed to see a screen and hear me and each other. At the convention center, I *had* double-checked about sufficient seating for the seminar attendees. At the client's building, I *had* checked with the meeting planner to ensure that the conference room would be available at my scheduled time. Sometimes things get lost in translation, or the meeting sponsor gives you all kinds of assurances either to keep you from worrying or to wrap up your phone call.

However, if your audience is uncomfortable, if the visuals cannot be seen, if the projector has a short, or if there is a strange odor in the room, you are the one responsible. It is in poor taste to blame the planner, the sponsor, the client, or anyone else. You are the one the audience counts on to take care of the details.

The best defense against such potential dilemmas and disasters lies in thorough planning. The site and surroundings can either make or break the ultimate impact of your message.

TIP 400: Use a Room, Facilities, and Equipment Checklist

As a presenter, keep a standard checklist of room, facility, and equipment features. For every presentation, check all items listed against your needs for that occasion. If the effort sounds like more detail than you can handle on your own, get help. Work closely with a logistic coordinator or sponsor to check out every possible glitch. Use a room, facilities, and equipment checklist to prevent last-minute problems.

Room/Facilities/Equipment Checklist

Client company: _____

Facility/location: _____

Room number: _____

Scheduler/coordinator: _____

Contact person in charge of problems: _____

ROOM
- ❏ Size and seating capacity
- ❏ Seating arrangement—classroom, chevron (V-shaped), theater; U-shaped
- ❏ Sight-line obstacles
- ❏ Location of speaker table
- ❏ Podium or raised dais
- ❏ Lighting and controls
- ❏ Window lighting and controls
- ❏ Window distractions
- ❏ Wall decor interfering with visuals placement or activities
- ❏ Temperature controls
- ❏ Pencil sharpener
- ❏ Clock
- ❏ Location of electrical outlets
- ❏ Two- or three-pronged outlets
- ❏ Water glasses and pitchers

(continued)

Room/Facilities/Equipment Checklist   (*Continued*)

FACILITIES

- ❏ Signs for arriving attendees
- ❏ Parking arrangements/charges
- ❏ Security requirements
- ❏ Appropriate entrances unlocked at all times
- ❏ Wheelchair access
- ❏ Restroom locations
- ❏ Water fountains
- ❏ Vending machines
- ❏ Snack areas
- ❏ Coat racks
- ❏ Smoking areas
- ❏ Copy machines
- ❏ Fax machines
- ❏ Phones for internal/external calls
- ❏ Stairs/elevator locations
- ❏ Fire-alarm procedures/drills planned

EQUIPMENT

Microphone:

- ❏ working lavaliere attachment
- ❏ extension cord for movement
- ❏ back-up batteries
- ❏ sound level
- ❏ taping to be done
- ❏ clicking sounds (such as jewelry hitting against the mike)

Flipchart:

- ❏ correct height
- ❏ enough paper
- ❏ working markers/right colors

Board:

- ❏ correct height
- ❏ clean surface
- ❏ working markers/right colors/erasable or permanent
- ❏ erasers
- ❏ cleaning solution

Overhead projector:

- ❏ spare bulbs
- ❏ focus knobs working
- ❏ extension cord
- ❏ clean surface
- ❏ pointer nearby

Slide projector:

- ❏ spare bulb
- ❏ focus knobs working
- ❏ tray cued to first slide
- ❏ order of slides
- ❏ remote control working
- ❏ projectionist to operate it

Room/Facilities/Equipment Checklist (*Continued*)

Multimedia system:
- ❑ projection screen in place
- ❑ video capabilities (imbedded video to be played from laptop projection system)
- ❑ audio capabilities (imbedded audio to be played from laptop projection system)
- ❑ extension cords
- ❑ remote control
- ❑ spare mouse
- ❑ laser pointer (if using)
- ❑ compatibility issues verified
- ❑ hand-held previewer
- ❑ list of file names for easy retrieval
- ❑ backup files or removable disks
- ❑ extra batteries (for pointer or remote control)
- ❑ adapters
- ❑ electrical cord for laptop
- ❑ charger for laptop battery
- ❑ cables between laptop and projector
- ❑ power strip
- ❑ surge protector
- ❑ external speakers (if house capabilities or projector audio not working)

VCR:
- ❑ size/type of cassette tape
- ❑ tape cued to appropriate place
- ❑ reset button working
- ❑ appropriate TV channel for access
- ❑ volume level
- ❑ working remote control
- ❑ outside interference

Projection screen(s):
- ❑ legs stable and sturdy
- ❑ located to project visuals at the appropriate size
- ❑ color of background easy to reflect
- ❑ pointer nearby
- ❑ visible to all attendees

Supplies:
- ❑ note pads
- ❑ pencils and pens or felt-tip markers
- ❑ blank transparencies
- ❑ name cards (size to be read from a distance)
- ❑ badges
- ❑ attendance sheets
- ❑ agenda or outline of session
- ❑ handouts, order blanks
- ❑ reference library
- ❑ demo objects
- ❑ cellophane tape (for paper)
- ❑ utility tape (for taping cords to the floor)
- ❑ pushpins or tacks
- ❑ rubber bands
- ❑ paper clips
- ❑ index cards
- ❑ clock for speaker
- ❑ visuals for speaker (such as time cues)
- ❑ extension cords

TIP 401: Arrive Early to Troubleshoot

Arriving on squealing tires is asking for trouble. Not only will you feel flustered, but so will your audience. And if they realize that you arrived just in the nick in the time, they will blame you profusely for anything at all that goes wrong—even those things you would have had no way to control had you arrived a *month* early.

TIP 402: Choose Your Microphone Carefully

In a small room, some presenters seem to pride themselves on shunning the microphone: "I don't think I need a mic—I project very well, can't you hear me in the back?" The audience nods, and the presenter continues without it. However, volume is not always the issue. A good microphone almost always will improve your voice quality.

Also, prefer a wireless lapel microphone whenever possible for maximum freedom—freedom to gesture with both hands simultaneously, freedom to walk without being limited by *X* feet of cord, freedom to walk away from the lectern.

Of course, you'll always need to use fresh batteries and check to see that you do not have interference from other microphones nearby.

TIP 403: Arrange Furniture and Equipment Facing Away from Windows and Doorways

Rebuild your "set" if necessary. You are in for an uphill battle if you are standing near the end of a conference room table and all the chairs are facing the hallway where everyone passes on the way to lunch. Own your presentation setting—not only where you intend to stand but where the audience will sit and look.

TIP 404: Remove Extra Chairs from the Room

Extra chairs tempt people to be dropouts. That is, with small groups, stragglers or those preoccupied with other tasks (such as cell phones) tend to sit away from the other attendees, making it more difficult for you to keep their attention and build rapport.

In large groups, extra chairs almost always ensure that the crowd will scatter—a cluster here, a cluster there, a few rows of eager participants toward the aisles and down front, and a few not-so-sure attendees on the outside edges and at the back. Again, this scattered crowd requires more energy from you to project your voice, makes it more difficult to build rapport with individuals, and decreases individuals' willingness to interact. When they are seated in isolated spots, they hesitate to respond to your requests for participation because they often feel as though they are responding alone rather than as part of a group.

There is another reason for the "no extra chairs" rule, however: If you have 400 chairs and 200 people show up, the impression created is that "nobody showed up." But if you have 100 chairs and 200 people show up (requiring you to set up extra chairs at the last minute), the impression created is that of "a full house." If this impression is important for your situation, consider the tradeoff to be worth the last-minute effort.

TIP 405: Provide an Exit Aisle to Create Comfort

Whatever the room size and arrangement, position the equipment and furniture so that there are exit aisles. People who feel trapped during presentations tend to grow resistant, even hostile, to the speaker and other attendees. Generally, an arrangement with only a few rows is preferable to many narrow rows because the wider format stimulates discussion.

TIP 406: Know When to Rise to the Occasion

To sit or stand on an elevated platform or riser—that is the question. Nothing irritates large audiences like having a presenter shun the platform provided and stand on the floor, where only those down front in the group can see movement, facial expressions, or gestures.

Yet it is understandable why presenters are inclined to go for the floor rather than rise to the occasion. In small groups, standing on a platform increases the "distance" between the presenter and the audience—both physically and psychologically. The farther away in space, the harder it is to build rapport—to have people look you in the eye, to see your gestures and facial expressions up close, to feel compelled to interact with you when you ask for responses.

So there is always a tradeoff between intimacy and annoyance—the intimacy of a small group being able to see you up close but the annoyance of those in large groups being unable to see you at all. Therefore, group size—not *your* comfort level—has to be the deciding factor.

And if you are standing behind a lectern (generally not a good idea), make sure you are tall enough to be seen by those in the front few rows (if you are on a platform) and by those in the back (if the lectern is on the floor). If the lectern blocks the audience's view, step away from it. You can always use a small table for notes or your laptop system.

TIP 407: Gather Your Group Closer to Aid in Control

If the room is too large for the group, and if the attendees are scattered throughout the room, ask them to move up front and closer together. Their proximity will make it easier for you to generate enthusiasm and maintain eye contact. Better yet, if possible, remove the extra chairs so that they have no choice.

TIP 408: Flash the Lights Off and On to Signal the Start of a Meeting

The unexpected flash will get the group's attention and signal that you are about ready to start your presentation. Allow a few seconds between the flash and your opening remarks to let them wind down their conversations and put away cell phones and paperwork.

TIP 409: Prevent Distractions by Posting "Do Not Disturb" Signs

You can be as assertive as you like with your signs, from "Do not disturb" signs in the center of the hallway outside to more subtly placed signs outside the door, "Session in progress." You also can add bulletin boards, message clips, or extension numbers for others to leave messages rather than come inside to interrupt your audience members.

13
Panache Despite Problems

You can pretend to be serious; you can't pretend to be witty.
SACHA GUITRY

Poor memory has its benefits. Otherwise a person would remember the times he has been a fool.
UNKNOWN

The easiest way to stay awake during an after-dinner speech is to deliver it.
HERMAN "PAT" HERST, JR.

Nobody ever thinks that bad things will happen to good presenters. Big mistake. Let's talk about working under less-than-desirable conditions. *What to Say When You're Dying on the Platform,* by Lilly Walters, is a wonderful book, chock full of humorous one-liners and helpful preventative tips for all those glitches that can fluster even the most experienced speaker.

DYING ON THE PLATFORM—WHEN A STORY OR HUMOR FLOPS

Jay Leno and David Letterman, the famed kings of nighttime TV, have a knack for turning a bomb into a bonanza by playing off a groaning rather than laughing audience. In fact, the legendary Johnny Carson made it his trademark. Most of us as presenters, however, will be far less favorably remembered for humor that flops.

TIP 410: Get Serious

Go with the flow. If you pause and no one reacts after the punch line, keep a straight face and make your serious point. You will have one, won't you?

TIP 411: Make Fun of Your Miss

If you cannot make the humor work as a serious point, try another one-liner to see if you can generate a smile or two after all. Here are some examples: "Strange—my mom thought it was hilarious." "Some of these stories I tell just for my own enjoyment." "That will grow on you." "If any of you laugh tomorrow, just remember that it was my comment about the X that brought it on."

FORGETTING/BECOMING FLUSTERED

Some goofs turn out to be funny—later, at least to the audience. Before a gathering of gregarious sales reps, I was trying to make the point that business communications are much less formal now than in past decades. "For example," I elaborated, "when you are introduced to someone, you rarely respond, 'How do you do?' Instead, you say something like, 'Hello' or 'Nice to meet you.' " Continuing this line of reasoning, I asked the group, "And when was the last time your family dressed formally to sit down at the dinner table together? Our family doesn't dress for dinner." One rep raised his hand and asked excitedly, "May we come?"

The audience roared with laughter; leaving me dumbfounded until someone in the front row pointed out to me what I'd said versus what I'd meant. Needlessly to say, after turning ten shades of red, I forgot where I was going with the next point.

TIP 412: Build a Mnemonic Device to Help You Recall Chunks

Memory experts tell us that our brains can hold only about seven chunks of information at once. For this reason, trying to remember 18 key points, six anecdotes, and three charts of data can be setting yourself up for disaster—unless you devise a better system of recall. Teachers have understood the value of mnemonic devices for ages. For example, piano teachers teach the scales EGBDF as *every good boy does fine*. Think of almost any discipline, and you will find technical concepts conveyed in models, mnemonics, and metaphors meant for easy recall. Create the same for yourself as a prevention tool.

TIP 413: Jump Ahead to a Key Anecdote That Serves as a Springboard

Stories stick better than an elaboration—even with the storyteller. In telling the story, you often will recall the point you typically make with the story by the time you get to the end of the story. And with that key point, the whole section of content will return to the forefront of your mind.

TIP 414: Fiddle with Fodder

Your fodder can be anything that fills a 10-second gap to provide you with thinking time to collect your thoughts. You may decide to take off or put on your eyeglasses so that you can "verify something." You may pause to take out your pen and jot a note while you regain your memory. You may stop speaking while you suddenly decide to move the flipchart back out of your walking space or erase a whiteboard of irrelevant information and then turn back again to face the group. You might stop to ask the group about the temperature—whether it is too warm or cool—and then ask someone in the back to adjust the thermostat.

Any of these breaks allow you 10 to 15 seconds—often all the time you need to recover your thoughts and continue. And often after such a movement it seems perfectly natural to ask the group, "Now where was I?" and they will help you out.

TIP 415: Change Locations in the Room

I have already mentioned that a location change to a speaker is like paragraphing to a writer. So it will seem quite natural to your audience that you would pause reflectively and stroll to another spot in the room to move to your next point. In the time it takes you to get there, you likely will have recovered from your memory lapse.

TIP 416: Code Your Visuals to Cue You

Use key words or subtitles to group sections of your visuals to keep you oriented by reminding you of the bigger context for an individual slide. With overhead transparencies, of course, you can write these key words on the frames as memory joggers.

When you are projecting from a laptop, a subtle color bar or icon in the corner or across the side or bottom will cue you about which segment of the presentation your visual belongs to. This highlighted color or icon, then, should trigger a complete chunk of information to the forefront of your mind. When you go out on a tangent with a detail and cannot find your way back, all you need to do is glance at the blue triangle to remind you that you are tracking the marketing goals for the second quarter. The orange triangle signals you that you are into third-quarter goals.

EQUIPMENT FAILURES

At a convention in New York City, I was 20 minutes into a presentation in which visuals played a key part when a power failure plunged us into total darkness for half an hour. A woman in the session began to scream that she was claustrophobic and darted toward the door, tripping over chairs and people in her path. Then the air conditioning went out. It was a very long half hour. With such mishaps, consider the following tips.

TIP 417: Prepare One-Liners for Various Equipment Problems That Occur Outside Your Control

Here are a few samples you may want to try:

Microphone Noise

"That was exactly what I said to my ex last week."

"Which is worse—that or my fingers-on-the-chalkboard trick?"

"Translated, that means, let's take a break."

"Okay, so somebody in the sound-control room doesn't agree with what I just said?"

Projector Goes Out

(*Pretending to read from a service tag on the equipment*) "Last serviced by Thomas Edison" (from speaker Tom Antion, Anchor Publishing).

"These slides may actually make more sense this way. What you don't see here is. . . ."

"I turned this thing on last Thursday morning—you'd think it would be warmed up by now."

Falling Equipment from Out of Sight

"Anybody hear that? Good. Then I'll just continue."

"Save the pieces. The guarantee's still good until 5 o'clock."

"I told him it might bite."

"We're about to try rearranging the furniture in here—anybody mind?"

TIP 418: Double-Check All Equipment—Never Assume That It Works

Never mind that you have just used the projector or the remote control the day before yesterday. Others may have changed settings, burned spare bulbs or batteries, or removed connections and forgotten to return them. However, the audience will blame *you* when things do not work and they must twiddle their thumbs while you chase down a solution.

STUMBLING, TRIPPING

I saw the cord. I moved the cord. I stepped over the cord. And then finally, I sprawled over the cord. Flat on my hands and face. And then again, poise and grace may have nothing to do with it. At a convention site in Minneapolis, I stepped off the platform and felt the two steps, not permanently attached by the hotel crew, collapse beneath me. In my state of embarrassment, a lawsuit seemed awfully tempting.

TIP 419: Tape All Cords to the Floor

This is the obvious thing that many fail to do, thinking they will remember the cords are there. (Guilty. See previous paragraphs.) Remembering *before* you start your presentation is quite different from remembering *after* you start.

TIP 420: Try Humor to Ease Embarrassment or Tension

My personal favorite: Jump up or straighten up quickly, glance around furtively as if to see if anyone is watching, and then ask, "Did anyone see that? Good." Their unease melts into laughter when they see that you are not hurt or devastated by the fall. Others have tried different lines with great success: "Just washed my feet and can't do a thing with them." Or "Did somebody just put that pole there?" Or "Did anybody see who loosened up that carpet on this side of the room when I wasn't looking?"

DISTRACTIONS

The sky's the limit when it comes to physical distractions—planes overhead, fire alarms, construction next door, messengers bringing in emergency announcements. Some you can control; others you cannot. Some are a combination of bad luck and your own doing.

Like the time I addressed a gathering of straitlaced financial people—the chief executive officer (CEO), president, and 17 executive vice presidents of an international banking system. Someone set a can of soda on my materials table when I was not looking. Ten minutes into my presentation, with one sweeping arm gesture, I knocked the can to the floor, splashing everything in its path as it puddled on the plush carpet of the executive meeting room.

The worst distraction occurred during a series of public seminars in a hotel in the Philippines. The setting was on the top floor of the hotel in a room with large windows on three sides. Twice a day a helicopter landed within 10 yards of our windows to pick up or deposit executives. The sound totally obliterated all voices for at least three to five minutes.

On another occasion, my client had a massive remodeling effort going on at corporate headquarters, with drills and buzz saws outside the door

**When Murphy's at work, try
humor to recapture attention.**

where I was conducting a training class. Did I mention that it was an oral presentation workshop, and we were trying to videotape the presenters?

Even the minor distractions, such as a ringing cell phone or groups of people entering and leaving a room next door or a retirement buffet down the hallway, tempt participants to disengage. Do all that you can to select a facility where you have control of such disruptions.

TIP 421: Call Attention to the Distraction, Regroup, and Regain Control

The cause of various out-of-control situations may be a freak incident, as in the following scenario: At a large meeting in a university auditorium, a page needed to deliver a message to the master of ceremonies. She edged through the curtains at the side of the stage and quietly made her way to the emcee, who was seated directly behind the speaker at the lectern. When the page gently touched the emcee on the shoulder, startled, he leaped from his chair with a loud scream. The audience roared, and the speaker at the lectern stopped abruptly, clueless about why the colleague behind him would spring from his chair with a yelp.

Naturally, after such incidents, you have to let the air clear before trying to regain control of the group. Once the laughter has died down, the noise has stopped, or the problem has been corrected, begin again in one of several ways.

You might recount a personal experience related to what just happened. Or simply acknowledge the interruption and then begin again. If you have forgotten where you were, ask the audience; they are bound to show sympathy and oblige you. Or simply recap your main points up to the interruption and continue.

TIP 422: Try Humor to Recapture Attention

Ringing Cell Phone (Yours or Someone Else's)

"Uh oh, forgot to tell my parole officer/parrot/grandmother where I was going."

"Must be difficult to be gone when you're the only one in the family/office who knows where they keep the getaway car."

"If that's the President (or your CEO), tell him I don't have time for his questions just now."

"Tell Mom I'll be sure to be home by nine."

"Tell him/her I'll bring the Jell-O."

Humorist Tom Antion, my friend and fellow speaker, has a great Web site at *www.publicspeaking.org* that provides great advice on humor and some witty one-liners such as these to handle ringing phones and many other such distractions.

TIP 423: Call a Break

Trying to talk through loud noise or a commotion is like trying to cut through a T-bone steak with a toothpick. You simply will not get through the barrier. If you clearly see that the group is no longer with you, either investigate the noise yourself or ask someone else to do so.

TIP 424: Talk About Mental Distractions

Mental distractions can be far worse than physical distractions—things such as a merger or layoff announced an hour before you are to make your presentation. I have had several such occasions: speaking to a group still reeling from the terrorist attacks at the World Trade Center, speaking to a group when their internal news broadcast has just released a story (unconfirmed and later proved to be false) that U.S. troops were under biological-chemical attack, and delivering a program to a group of managers when they were being randomly called out of my session and laid off.

In such situations, you may be talking, but few people will be listening—unless you go find them mentally and emotionally. That is, they are frozen in place at the point of distraction.

You will need to move to where they are psychologically. Acknowledge their situation by talking about it and giving the group a chance to air feelings and opinions. Then, once they have traded views, opinions, and emotions, they will much more readily "wind down" and give you their attention as an escape from the stress of the current situation.

SIDE CONVERSATIONS

Side conversations present another challenge. Members of your audience may talk to each other for any number of reasons. Someone arrives late and asks a colleague for an update. Perhaps the customer's technical representative wants to know where to find your diagrams in the printout. Or someone complains to a colleague that the room is too hot or cold. If audience members' energy is flagging, maybe they need a break. Or the person talking disagrees with you and wants others to know it.

If you can determine the reason for a side conversation, you can handle it more appropriately.

TIP 425: Ignore Helpful Distractions

If someone explains something to a peer or "catches up" a late arriver and the conversation gives signs of coming to an end, try to ignore the distraction. In fact, the person engaged may be saving the larger group the distraction of a "replay" should the confused person ask you questions personally.

TIP 426: Acknowledge the Body Language of Those Who Disagree

Many side conversations erupt from disagreement left to smolder under the surface. If audience members make it a point with their body language to tell you they disagree—obvious head wagging, disgusted shuffling in their seats, glancing around the room trying to catch others' eyes— they are dangerously close to exploding verbally.

If the talker wants to express an opposing view, offer that opportunity or at least acknowledge that position: "I know that some of you have experiences and ideas to the contrary, and you'll be welcome to express those at the end of the presentation." Such comments remove the urge for these naysayers to begin their comments too early to those seated nearby.

TIP 427: Stroll Closer to the Talkers Without Looking at Them

If you can tell two people are simply catching up on corporate gossip or chatting about personal issues, stroll in their direction as you speak—but without looking at them specifically. As all eyes follow your movement and as your voice grows louder and louder in their ears, the talkers will soon feel all attention focused on them, a pressure tactic that usually stops such conversations.

TIP 428: Call for More Audience Involvement

If you suspect that your talkers have lost interest in your presentation, change your game plan and call for more audience involvement. Take an opinion poll on your current point and reflect on the results. A moment for input and open discussion from everyone generally will break up the small pockets of side conversations as they tune in to see what they are missing from their colleagues.

LATECOMERS

They are late to arrive and late to return from breaks. Never hold or stop your presentation to accommodate them or you will lose the rest of your group. Always start on time, letting latecomers ask others what they missed later. Otherwise, you will "train" your attendees that you do not mean what you say about the stop and start times. In fact, some organizations have "trained" their entire employee population not to take meeting start times or training class times seriously.

TIP 429: Use a Buffer If You Must

On certain occasions, you may decide to deviate from the start-on-time rule so that a key decision maker who is still out of the room does not miss an important point. A good technique for "having it both ways" is to begin the session on time but start with a buffer (such as cartoons or a humorous anecdote related to your point) so that the latecomer arrives in time to hear your "real" topic opening.

TIP 430: Use a Common Clock

When announcing a break, clearly state the restart time and point to the wall clock; this helps attendees remember the time better. Or rather than giving an exact time to return and confuse everyone whose watch is not synched with yours, state: "Please look at your watches. We'll start the presentation again in 12 minutes."

TIP 431: Provide Incentives

Give the audience something to look forward to immediately after a break. Examples: Promise to share "the inside scoop" on some company issue; consider taking an opinion poll right before a break and announcing and interpreting the results immediately afterwards; draw for prizes—door prizes, contest prizes, or brainteaser prizes; or show funny photos of the crowd.

TIP 432: Remove the Dropout Zone

Having extra empty chairs at the back of the room for latecomers solves the distraction problem for the short term but prolongs it for the long term. Those who arrive late at the beginning or late after breaks can sit there and not traipse down front, distracting everyone in the middle of your presentation. On the other hand, in the long run, others observe that latecomers are accommodated—that these extra chairs remain at the back and allow attendees to arrive late and leave early with minimal (they think) distraction. So as the session drags on, more and more people do just that—arrive late and take a seat in the dropout zone.

HECKLERS IN THE CHEAP SEATS

Generally, hecklers who create a real distraction gain the hostility of the group and provoke sympathy for you. I am defining hecklers here in two ways: (1) those outside your organization and (2) the cynics some supervisor sent in his or her absence "to make sure X doesn't get approved without our input." The following tips will be more appropriate to the first group than the latter.

TIP 433: Move Physically Closer to Them Before Your Session Begins

Your tendency may be to do the opposite. Making direct eye contact, approaching them, and courteously asking why they are protesting your presentation may defuse their hostility. At the least, your sincere approach will decrease the probability that they will be rude to you personally—even if they never consider changing their views.

TIP 434: Move Away from Them After Your Session Begins

If the hecklers are to the side or otherwise visible to the audience, casually move in the opposite direction so that the eyes of the audience members will follow you, and the hecklers will drop out of their line of vision.

TIP 435: Ignore Them If You Can

If they gain the group's attention, speak directly to them, calling attention to the fact that the others came to hear your views.

TIP 436: Unmask Them

If you are expecting a hostile audience and protocol dictates that you must allow them the floor, you can always ask attendees for their names, titles, and organizational affiliations at the beginning of the presentation. Having lost their anonymity and chancing repercussions from their organization or embarrassment for their family, they are often hesitant to express their hostility openly.

TIP 437: Control the Microphone and Attention

You typically can end any dialogue with this comment: "There are individuals and groups who may see things very differently. I can accept that. I hope they can." Then move on with your presentation in a dynamic way. Under no condition should you give the microphone to hecklers. Never ask them a question and give them the opportunity to state their views to the crowd or put you on the defensive.

Remember that audiences will follow your lead.

Whatever the problem—preventable or otherwise—most audiences are forgiving and sympathetic. Goofs remind them that you are human, have weaknesses, get flustered, make mistakes, and experience frustrating circumstances and challenges—all of which make you seem more like them.

If you treat an incident as a major setback, the group may focus on it and become annoyed at you or the circumstance, to the point of minimizing your ideas and information. On the other hand, if you apologize, downplay the distraction, regain your composure, and correct the problem quickly, they will just as quickly revert to their previously attentive mode.

Problems—both those you can and cannot control—will happen. Do everything you can to prevent and minimize their impact. Then relax and take surprises in stride. Who says speaking before a group isn't adventurous?

14

Emceeing—Tying It All Together

America needs more free speech that is worth listening to.   UNKNOWN

Some people are so intelligent they can speak on any subject—others don't seem to need a subject.   UNKNOWN

Some of the driest speeches are made by people who are all wet.   UNKNOWN

Most politicians have four speeches: what they have written down, what they actually say, what they wish they had said, and what they are quoted as saying the next day.   UNKNOWN

A good emcee functions much like a home page for a Web site. The emcee greets the audience members, grabs their attention, overviews succinctly what the program is all about, establishes credentials, serves as the thread of continuity, provides transitions between extended presentations, and sums up with sponsor and contact information, along with the appropriate "thank yous." In short, being a master of ceremonies takes skill and preparation.

UNDERSTANDING YOUR ROLE AND IDENTIFYING YOUR TASKS

TIP 438: Understand the Image You Are to Create

Why have you been asked to serve as emcee? Is the sponsor expecting a stand-up comic or a more serious business presence? What have previous emcees done to be effective? What has displeased previous sponsors and audiences? Plan your comments accordingly.

TIP 439: Know Your Responsibilities Regarding the Logistics

Must you follow a strict time frame? Some programs are timed to the minute and even half minute, with audiovisual people standing by to show video clips at 9:04 and music cued to begin at 9:05:30. Are you responsible to write introductions for panelists or speakers, or will those be provided? Are you responsible to speak to servers about silent service as they clear tables? Or should you wait until meal service is completed to begin? Who will help you draw for and award any door prices? Are you expected to ask sponsors to donate door prizes? Are you expected to be a judge in any contests? Will the audience have printed programs with the time frames and speaker biographies included?

TIP 440: Coordinate with Panelists or Speakers Ahead of Time

Take the mystery out of the muse for all concerned by setting up a conference call prior to the event—far enough in advance so that your panelists or speakers have not already finished their preparation. Let them introduce themselves to each other and give a brief overview of their topics. Then, during this time, explain to them the time restrictions and how you will handle any questions or interaction with the audience. You can ask them to tell you or send you questions they would like to be asked.

Here are other key issues to coordinate during this phone call: Will they all speak first and then all take questions? Will you stop for questions between speakers? Will you ask the same questions of all panelists? Will each panelist respond to every question? How should they signal you if they want to add something to what another panelist says or if they do not want to respond to a question at all? Such planning will accomplish several things: It will tend to eliminate repetition in their comments. It will let them know that you are serious about time limits. It will signal them that you expect preparation, not just off-the-cuff drivel. It will put them at ease in knowing you want to help them shine.

TIP 441: Prepare a Strong Opening

Create excitement about the program. Tell the audience what you expect they will get out of the session—laughter, networking, business ideas, recognition for a job well done, or an opportunity to hear strategic objectives, investigate controversial issues with experts, or accomplish the stated meeting goals.

Often you can tie the occasion to a current event either in the life of the organization, the city, or the international community.

TIP 442: Provide a Thread of Continuity and a Context

As you listen to various speakers or panelists, look for commonalities. Take notes on what they say so that you can *very briefly* reemphasize points you especially agree with and relate their key points to what is coming up next. Your comments do not have to be particularly witty or meaningful. They just have to weave the audience's thought process from point A to point B in the program.

TIP 443: Prepare Clever Ad Libs for Glitches

Unless you have locked Murphy in the closet for the evening, you can expect a few things to go as unplanned: malfunctioning equipment, late food service, loud outside noise, a late-arriving speaker, or a VIP who could not attend at the last moment. Have some witty one-liners to deliver "spontaneously" when such things happen. See Chapter 13 for examples.

TIP 444: Work the Crowd

The most skilled emcees take their chances in working the crowd—Leno, Letterman, and Oprah style. For example, after a panelist speaks, you might ask the audience, "How many of you were surprised by those statistics on X?" or "Anybody here have a follow-up question to those remarks?" and then take the microphone to that audience member for the question. Or walk through the crowd to ask for personal experiences that illustrate the speaker's last point. Or ask the crowd if anyone has found a workable solution to the issues raised by the speaker?

And you can always do quick surveys with a show of hands. For example, if the speaker has been talking about taxation on small businesses, you might ask, "How many of you as small business owners have had your property taxes increased in this last year?" "For how many of you has it gone up more than 20 percent?" Such interactions with the audience serve to create a sense of community, provide context for the group, and customize a speaker's message for your specific audience.

TIP 445: Prepare a Strong Close

If you would like, add your own brief comments, reemphasizing the theme and purpose of the program or event. Then tie up all the loose ends. Thank the appropriate people.

INTRODUCING OTHERS

Because introducing others is a large part of the emceeing role, you will want to devote special attention to this responsibility. A good introduction—yours or others—should be no longer than a minute or two. Otherwise, you or they should have published a biography in the printed program.

TIP 446: Collect Information on the Speakers That Will
Establish Credibility and Be Relevant to a Specific Audience

The speaker cannot afford to take precious presentation time to cite his or her degrees, certifications, accomplishments, and experience. And even if there were time, most would be too modest to do so. Yet credibility is crucial for an audience to accept a presenter's message from the get-go. Your job as introducer is to reduce that credibility gap in two ways: presenting both the formal and informal credentials.

The informal ones include the facts important to a specific group—details that will make the audience identify with and like the speaker as a person. People believe people they like. Most audience members will not have time to meet the speakers individually. This is why you so often hear emcees comment on friendly conversations they have just had with the speaker before the meeting, over dinner, or during the program-planning phase. In short, they are saying, "She's a nice person; trust me on this." And most audiences do just that.

TIP 447: Create an Air of Intrigue About the
Speaker's Topic

Like the appetizer, it is your job to whet the audience's appetite for the main course. You may tell them briefly why it is important, why the speaker's perspective may be unique, or what you expect the audience will gain from the presentation. Take care, however, that you do not overdo it here and steal the speaker's own introduction to the topic. Like good hors d'oeuvres, you want to provide just a bite or two, not fill the audience to capacity so that they no have no appetite for the main event.

TIP 448: Consider Your Introduction a Minipresentation

Even if just a minute or two, your introduction should have an attention-getting introduction, a body of key points or facts tied together with transitions, and a sizzling summary that motivates the audience to "listen up." It should be a cohesive whole, not just a recitation of facts.

TIP 449: Be Conversational Rather than Formal and Stilted

Learn your key points and know the facts, but do not memorize the introduction verbatim. Otherwise, it sounds too formal and often canned. (Many professional speakers, however, do provide their introducers with a written introduction as a go-by because they have suffered through so many poor introductions from emcees who never take the time to prepare.) Your intention with an introduction is to lend warmth and a personal endorsement for what is to come. If you are not excited enough about the person to know the facts and be able to relate them, the audience will interpret, "No big deal."

TIP 450: Pronounce the Speaker's Name Correctly

Writing difficult names phonetically often helps. When you are nervous, memory can even make Sam Smith or Jill Jones seem tentative. If in doubt, don't. Just ask. Speakers want you to say their name correctly.

TIP 451: Pronounce the Speaker's Name Last as You Give the Floor to Him or Her and Lead the Applause

Build to the grand finale—the speaker's name. Lead the applause, wait to welcome him or her to the stage or lectern, and then take your seat.

INTRODUCING YOURSELF

TIP 452: Provide Credentials in Print

> A brief introduction in a printed program, on a handout, or on a visual is the best alternative when you do not have a live "third party" introducer.

TIP 453: Walk the Tightrope Between Credibility and Commonality

> Generally, it is better to introduce yourself *as* you speak rather than *before* you speak. That is, rather than providing all the details at once up front, weave them in as you go. Granted, people need to believe that you know what you are talking about, and that requires that they know about certain credentials. However, stated too early, they sound like braggadocio. Stated too late, you are playing "catch-up" because your audience may have already tuned out and discarded much of what you have said—particularly if what you have to say is controversial.
>
> In cases where you cannot provide credentials ahead of time and must introduce yourself from the platform, keep commonality in the forefront of your mind. Other than giving your name, focus your enthusiasm on the program, the event, any awards, the cause, honored guests, or the other speakers.
>
> Then gradually, as you move through the program, you will have opportunity to insert a few facts about yourself here and there—such as organizational affiliation, area of expertise, why they asked you to do the honors of emceeing, and so forth. By the end of the evening, the audience will have the full picture of who you are—without your having to hit them over the head with the facts. And in the meantime, you will have come across as "one of the them," establishing a common bond of trust.

15
Audio- and Videoconferencing— When You're "Live but Not in Person"

If you don't double click me, I can't do any-
thing.   JOHN ANISTON

It has become appallingly obvious that our tech-
nology has exceeded our humanity.
                                ALBERT EINSTEIN

Live TV died in the late 1950s, electronic bul-
letin boards came along in the mid-1980s,
meaning there was about a 25-year gap when it
was difficult to put your foot in your mouth and
have people all across the country know about it.
                                 MARK LEEPER

You can do almost anything in a videoconference that you can do in person—lecture, discuss, create visuals, display graphics, demonstrate things.
You simply have to do them a little differently. This difference in setting and
equipment requires that you give more forethought and planning to the
hows of your presentation. The convenience and savings of time and travel
expense far outweigh the effort invested in learning to use your equipment
properly and planning your presentation.

BEFORE YOU GO LIVE

TIP 454: Determine Your Purpose

The purpose of your videoconference should dictate how to proceed: to share information from a single source or between several sites, to present goals and then discuss implementation ideas, to present a problem for decision, to motivate people to take action, or to gather input from your participants.

TIP 455: Set the Equipment and Room for Your Specific Goals

At the end of the conference, what will participants know, feel, or do? More important, what methods will you use to arrive at that goal? Arrange the overall setup with this purpose in mind.

TIP 456: Consider Different Time Zones

When you announce meeting times, be sure to state the time zone. It is easy for participants to become confused when the meeting leader announces a time in his or her local time zone and then the site manager sends out an extra e-mail or note with the local time, accompanied by the announced times from the host site.

TIP 457: Give Careful Attention to Room Setup

Avoid rooms with predominately white and dark colors because they create unnatural-looking skin tones. Avoid wild patterns in drapes, murals, carpets, or upholstery of chairs. Remove art or other framed objects with reflective surfaces that may cause glare. Cover distracting, glaring images you cannot remove with an off-white or pastel tablecloth or drape.

Ideally, lighting should come from multiple sources around the room. Point lights away from the cameras and monitors to avoid glare and "washing out" images. Light the back wall to provide a good contrast in the participant images.

Display a banner on the table or wall that identifies the various sites as they appear on camera. Provide tent cards to set in front of participants (easier to read in group shots) and nametags for participants to wear (easier to read in close-up shots).

Make sure each site has a clock.

Have backup batteries for the wireless control units at each site.

TIP 458: Pay Particular Attention to the Seating Arrangement

Allow each person three to four feet at the table. A camera 10 to 11 feet away can frame three people in a shot. Viewers should be seated at a distance from the screen that is between four to seven times the height of the viewing monitor in the room.

Prefer to have people face the camera rather than face each other to encourage interaction between sites. There are two preferred seating arrangements for best interaction: (1) Have participants sit in the arc of an oval on one side of the table. They can then see the monitor and each other (at least better than sitting shoulder to shoulder). (2) Have participants sit at the corner of a rectangular table, with two on one side of the corner and two on the other side of the corner. In either arrangement, when the participants are on camera, they will all appear to be facing the other sites, yet they can still see and hear each other at the local site.

TIP 459: Practice with the Equipment Before Presentation Time

Familiarize yourself with the meeting equipment and mechanics included here if you will be responsible for controlling the videoconferencing system without assistance from other technicians. Otherwise, participants may be hearing a voice but seeing no face.

TIP 460: Plan a Live Equipment and Lighting Check

As participants arrive for the videoconference, check equipment with them. Heating or air-conditioning systems may create distracting noise. Lighting requires special attention. Window drapes may need to be closed. Participants should not sit in front of a window or other bright object such as a picture frame that will cause a silhouette effect. You as presenter will need plenty of light on your face, yet too much light coming from directly above will create a "raccoon" effect around your eyes.

Verify that all microphones and cameras are plugged in, have batteries, or are operating properly.

TIP 461: Know When to Use Close-Ups and Group Shots

Use close-up shots when you are giving your presentation or when someone is asking or answering a question. Use close-up shots of yourself to regain control. Use wide shots when no one in particular is speaking at a single site but when you want to try to "reduce the distance" between groups and create awareness of other participants. Also, vary shots between close-ups and wide shots to minimize the feeling of distance and isolation and to give the sense of "moving along" in the meeting.

TIP 462: Plan When to Use Voice-Activated Control Versus Director Control

Use voice-activated mode when you want to encourage discussion and input. Use director control when you want to reestablish control, move to a new topic, or handle a disagreement between sites or people. Use director control when displaying a graphic or showing a video; otherwise, a loud sound at a remote site will switch the picture to the site and off your graphic or video.

TIP 463: Number Your Visuals

It is much easier for the camera operator, and even yourself if you are operating the document camera, to refer quickly to visuals by numbers (slide 4, diagram of the building) rather than by topics or titles alone. Also, numbering visuals allows you to refer to them more easily in sites where participants may have a technical glitch and may be seeing only hard copy.

TIP 464: Use a Graphic Font Size of 36 Points or Larger

This font size for text is a good rule of thumb for projected slides in any case but a necessity for videoconferencing. Anything smaller will be unreadable.

TIP 465: Size Your Graphics Appropriately and Check Resolution

Your visuals must be in landscape format to match the videoconferencing monitor ratio. Allow margins that are 10 to 15 percent of the image size of your graphic. Use no more than six lines per screen. Save details for a handout. You can use computer-generated graphics with no problem, but be sure to check resolution quality. Video-monitor resolution is much lower than computer-monitor resolution; what looks great on your computer screen may appear fuzzy on the videoconference screen. When using white-boards and hand-printed graphics, consider the glare. Use pastel or off-white paper and a blue broad-tip pen.

TIP 466: Prepare Audience-Involvement Questions

To encourage discussion, have prepared questions to stimulate thought and response and to move the group toward accomplishing the purpose. When discussion careens out of control, guide with focused questions.

TIP 467: Plan Change-of-Pace Activities

For an idea of frequency, watch television network news broadcasts and count how many times there's a change of visuals during coverage of one single news broadcast. Plan your own presentation accordingly. Consider adding graphics, interactive surveys, discussion questions, site breakout activities, interviews with experts, reports, or video clips to keep the participants' interest. Remember that they will be comparing your broadcast to what they see daily on major television networks.

TIP 468: Dress with the Camera and Lighting Situation in Mind

Avoid patterned fabrics such as large prints, dots, plaids, and stripes, all of which may "dance" on the screen. Camera lenses also have difficulty balancing certain extreme colors such as black and white. And occasionally, red "bleeds." For shirts and blouses, prefer pastels rather than white. Medium-dark colors at the center of the spectrum package you best: royal blue, purple, burgundy, navy, green, or charcoal gray. Avoid scarves, ruffles, complex-pattern ties, or fabrics that rustle or jewelry that clanks when you move.

If you wear glasses, touch the frames with powder to tone down the shine. In fact, avoid any reflective accessory such as a tie clasp, earrings, or brooch that "stands out." You want the audience to remember you and your message, not the necktie or necklace.

If you are going to be on camera as presenter for an extended period of time, use makeup to avoid appearing unnatural—sickly, weak, nervous.

However, the idea is to look natural. This means that you should avoid bright, shimmering colors in lipsticks and eye shadows and strong blush, which the camera will "play with" to your disadvantage. Powder any shines on the forehead, nose, and chin. Cover dark circles or shadows under the eyes, which will be even darker on camera.

AFTER YOU GO LIVE

TIP 469: Display a Welcome Visual as Remote Participants Come Online

As presenter, consider yourself the host. Provide the date, meeting time (and time zone), host site, and participating sites.

TIP 470: Introduce Yourself and Other Participants

In addition to introducing yourself and any other participants at your site, include support staff or technicians and their roles in the meeting or broadcast. Then have other sites introduce their participants, support staff, and observers along with their roles. You may find it helpful to appoint a chairperson at each site to handle the introductions and administrative tasks. Mention if you will be audiotaping or videotaping the meeting and the procedures for getting copies of the tape after the session.

TIP 471: Review Any Guidelines or Ground Rules That Will Increase Productivity

For example, remind people about the pause before or after speaking. Encourage those who will be speaking for longer periods—such as during your question-and-answer period or during other planned interactivity—to say when they have finished with their remarks so that others know this quickly. Also, to avoid confusion, remind participants to identify themselves and their site when they speak.

TIP 472: Identify Yourself When You Speak

For example, "This is Kevin in Miami. I have a question for the New Orleans site . . ." helps to orient everyone quickly. Ask all participants to identify themselves each time they speak because in large groups it is easy to lose the thread of a conversation when several voices may sound alike. The only exception from these repeated identifications is the primary presenter or host.

TIP 473: Speak in a Normal Tone and Volume— Your Best

The microphones are sensitive, so there is no need to lean forward toward a microphone or raise your voice.

TIP 474: Be Mindful of Slight Audio Delays

Pause longer than usual to allow others to respond before you continue. When someone else is speaking, wait to make sure that he or she has finished before you respond, add your own comments, or change topics.

TIP 475: Make Sure That You Are Facing the Online Camera When You Speak

Remember that you are not simply presenting to others around the conference table or in your room. Prefer to make eye contact via the camera with other sites than with those seated around you. If there are multiple cameras, check the TV monitor to make sure that you are facing the camera that is currently online. And make sure that you are completely within the camera's field of vision as you speak.

TIP 476: Be Mindful of the Ever-Present Camera and the Open, Sensitive Microphone

Be careful that you are not inadvertently calling attention to your movement by shuffling papers, strumming fingers, swiveling chair, coughing, sighing and harrumphing, tapping pen or pointer or water glass, or snacking. Several water glass clanks on a hard table can sound like a hailstorm at another site. Also, give attention to posture. Just because you cannot see your audience during a broadcast does not mean that they cannot see you. Avoid unconscious mannerisms such as rubbing your eyes, tossing your hair back, flipping your tie, or twirling a pencil.

TIP 477: Become Familiar with the Mute Button and Use It Often

Because microphones are very sensitive, it is a good idea to mute the audio at any time that you are not speaking to eliminate all extraneous noise: air conditioners coming on and off, background conversations, projector noise, rustling paper, pencil tapping, coughing, or throat clearing.

TIP 478: Be Careful About Sudden Moves Toward the Camera

Extending your hands, flailing your arms, shifting your weight, crossing your legs—such movements look aggressive and even make your hands or arms look much larger as they plunge forward. The camera greatly exaggerates wide, sweeping gestures and pointing fingers and may make you look hysterical rather than authoritative.

TIP 479: Be Mindful of Exaggerated Negative Expressions

Many people notice that they have a rather stern look on camera. When you are used to the warm feedback and encouraging nods of a live audience six feet in front of you instead of a cold camera, you tend to become mechanical yourself. Be aware that gestures and facial expressions are exaggerated on camera. A scowl may seem overly harsh and disapproving.

To lighten up your facial expressions, think how you appear when you are slightly amused. That is, raise your eyebrows slightly and keep your gaze and chin turned slightly upward. Caress the camera with your eyes to show sincerity and warmth. Or try to visualize the camera as a colleague sitting directly in front of you, nodding or raising an eyebrow at everything you say.

TIP 480: Be Extra Mindful of Vocal Variety

Vary your speech patterns and voice—fast and slow rate of speaking, high and low pitch, loud and soft volume, inflection, emphasis, and intonation. While important during in-person presentations, vocal variety becomes crucial in videoconferencing. A monotonous presentation online puts people to sleep.

TIP 481: Break Long Monologues into Shorter Chunks

Unlike face-to-face conversations, where others can signal with body language that they want the floor, participants grow even more impatient because they feel helplessly trapped listening to a monologue without opportunity for comment or question. Such reminders particularly serve a purpose when some systems allow only one speaker at a time. With those systems, others literally cannot interrupt.

TIP 482: Consider People as Participants, Not Passive Viewers

Even when you are primarily sharing information from a single site, let participants know from time to time that you are mindful that they are "out there." As much as possible, make them true participants rather than simply passive viewers. Plan some early interaction so that they feel a part of the group from the beginning.

TIP 483: Encourage Communication Between Two Sites

Toss out questions or issues and permit participants to discuss them among sites and to ask questions of other sites without directing all interactions back to you: Do ask them to identify themselves as they speak, but avoid having participants consider you as traffic cop for the interactions. Lead and control, but do not stifle interaction.

TIP 484: Respond to Questions with Complete Sentences

Avoid one-word or phrase responses because of the audio delays.

TIP 485: Be Briefer Than in Traditional Settings

In general, virtual presentations should be shorter than traditional ones because it is more difficult to hold participants' attention. Remember that switching between sites takes longer than a continual presentation from one person at one site. Remember also that discussion and feedback segments are more difficult to time than presentations given to an on-site audience.

Allow breaks every hour. If your storyboard reveals that a meeting probably will last longer than available airtime, rethink your plans. Consider these options: Cut some topics. Revise your methods to have less interactivity. Divide your topics into two or more presentations.

TIP 486: Plan Post-Videoconference Work and Communication

While participants are together at each site, do you want the participants to discuss the specifics of how to implement a decision at their local site? Do you need to ask all participants to forward information to a specific place after the videoconference? Give such instructions while you are still on the air and while people at each site are still together.

TIP 487: Conclude with Purpose and Direction

Do not let your presentation and meeting whimper to a close with participants and sites simply drifting away. Thank people for their participation and restate how to get audio or video copies of your presentation in its entirety. Finally, design a way to collect feedback on your presentation so that you can evaluate and improve its effectiveness.

Videoconferencing increases productivity, saves travel time and money, and contributes to a team-building culture. Use the equipment and adapt your presentation and speaking style to take full advantage of the medium.

NOTE: The dos and don'ts above may vary with (or may not be applicable to) your particular videoconferencing and audioconferencing equipment and room setup such as number, angle, and activation of cameras; the number of monitors; the audio quality; available peripherals (computers, scanners, faxes, printers, whiteboards, and audio and video recorders); and reliability of operation.

16
Evaluating Results—
Turning Success or Failure
into Fire in the Belly

*Second wind is what some preachers get when
they say, "And now in conclusion."*
UNKNOWN

No speech is entirely bad if it's short enough.
UNKNOWN

*A good speech is one with a good beginning and
a good ending, which are kept very close
together.*
UNKNOWN

Ultimately, our audience has the last say about our effectiveness. In the interim, however, we have opportunity to evaluate ourselves and ask others to provide critique and coaching. The helpfulness of that coaching is directly proportional to whom you ask and how you ask.

You can turn failure into fire—fire in the belly for success. Every powerful presentation leaves you panting for another opportunity to take the platform. Every failure can leave you determined to correct the false step. The difference between the smell of victory and the taste of defeat is often personal evaluation and colleague coaching.

TIP 488: Record Every Presentation You Give to Evaluate It

We tend to remember only our best or worst: When the auditorium thunders with applause—or when attendees get up and walk out in disgust. When the boss stands up from the conference table, exits the meeting with glowing remarks, and lets us know a promotion will be coming our way—or reminds us in a performance appraisal a year later about the presentation fiasco. When the sales presentation ends with the client signing on the dotted line—or ends the relationship.

To get a true picture of our *typical* presentation style, however, we need not be overly focused on the outward results that may or may not have happened because of our poise, pizzazz, or persuasion.

For a more in-depth evaluation, study your presentation style in a variety of settings with diverse groups on different topics.

TIP 489: Record Yourself on Video to Study Your Gestures, Posture, and Movement

The old saying "The camera doesn't lie" has become a cliché for good reason. Turn off the audio, and study only the visual to focus on that part of your presentation skills.

TIP 490: Record Yourself Only on Audio to Focus on Vocal Improvement

Given a choice of listening to a ball game over the radio or watching it on television, the vast majority would prefer to watch it. It only stands to reason, then, that if you intend to critique your voice while you are watching yourself on video, what you see will overpower what you hear.

When listening to yourself on audio alone, those vocal "tics" stand out more prominently—dropped word endings, unfinished sentences, rapid-fire speaking rate, words fillers such as *uhs* and *ahs,* or a monotone.

Awareness itself goes a long way toward self-improvement.

TIP 491: Start with Your Greatest Detractor

Are there one or two things that all your coaches or you yourself notice above all others as negatives? Poor eye contact? A rigid posture? Disorganized content? A monotone? If you could only improve one or two things, what should they be? Focus on those one or two things to the exclusion of all else. As with any other skill, you cannot improve everything at once. Move to the areas of greatest weakness and remove those one by one. Your audiences will notice an immediate improvement, and your self-confidence will soar.

TIP 492: Look for What You Do Well and Become Masterful

Are you great at ad-libbing funny lines during the question-and-answer session? If so, do it more often during the prepared section of your content. Can you think of several creative, attention-getting openings? If so, then work more "grabbers" into all the key points of your talk. If you have strong natural gestures, work on using them more often and making them content-specific.

Working to build on your strengths is the fun part of practice. Ask the Olympic champions, professional athletes, movie stars, and recording artists.

TIP 493: Tell Coaches What Kind of Feedback You Need

"Listen to this presentation and tell me what you think" is little better than asking for no critique at all. Are you really asking for reassurance on what you have worked on for so long? Or do you want ideas for additional content? Do you want them to find something that you are doing wrong—no matter how small—so that they have something to tell you? Or would you like them to point out what you are doing effectively as well? Are you asking if your presentation structure *flows clearly and seems logical* to them? Are you asking if the information *interests* them? Are you asking if the information is *new or valuable* to them? Are you asking if they think the *intended audience* will value the presentation? Are you asking if your delivery style is adequate? Are you asking if your delivery style is dynamic? Compared to what standard?

Coaches cannot provide what they do not understand you to be asking. Tell them exactly what kinds of feedback you want, what your standards are, and how specific you would like them to be.

TIP 494: Accept Feedback Without Defensiveness

If you have asked others for their evaluative comments, then you have committed yourself to listen. This does not mean that you have to agree. However, courtesy dictates that you accept the comments you solicited without a defensive tone, without rationalizing or explaining why you needed to do this or that.

Open, helpful responses may include some of these: "Tell me more." "Can you clarify for me?" "Can you recall a few specific examples of that?" "Do you have suggestions of how to improve or change that?"

Invite elaboration. Make notes. Thank your coach. Reflect before you decide whether to act on the feedback or discard it.

TIP 495: Go with the Numbers on Subjective Issues

Remember that critique is subjective. If you have feedback from five people and one says a particular mannerism is distracting but others do not even notice it, go with the majority. On the other hand, in some cases it may be that the one individual is more perceptive than others. For example, four individuals may tell you that you do not look confident, but only one coach can tell you exactly why—that your eyes keep darting up toward the left. That one person's insight about why others may consider you nervous may be very helpful.

TIP 496: Don't Ask Highly Critical Colleagues for Feedback

Either wait until you are very confident of your abilities to ask for feedback from your most highly critical colleagues or family members or do not ask at all. When you ask for critique from some people, they consider the assignment to mean "Tell me what I'm doing wrong" rather than "Tell me what's effective and what's not." Consequently, they focus only on the negative. And their evaluation can devastate you—especially a day or two before an important presentation.

Prefer instead to ask for feedback from someone who will give a more balanced evaluation—both strengths and areas for improvement.

TIP 497: Observe Other Speakers to Learn from Them

You will learn what works and what does not by watching others present and, more important, by watching the reaction they generate from the audience. I've not met a speaker yet from whom I couldn't learn something.

Epilogue:
So You're Up Now

The way you speak—I think we're going to have to move you into a more visible position in the company. How about the new title of _____, at a $50,000 increase?

Powerfully persuasive. I'm ready to sign on the dotted line!

Your presentation changed my life. I'll never be the same because of you.

Your comments were right on target—I share your thoughts and values completely.

Your talk was so moving, you had people weeping. They were enthralled.

Visualize yourself getting comments such as these from appreciative audiences routinely. Actually receiving such remarks makes all the preparation and prespeaking jitters worthwhile. There are few things more satisfying than knowing you have influenced others to your way of thinking—whether it is to buy a particular product or to change the course of their lives.

Yes, you can do it. With your new bag of tricks and techniques, go ahead and speak up with confidence!

List of Tips

Tip 1: Establish Integrity Through Third-Party Endorsements

Tip 2: Be Genuine

Tip 3: Show Enthusiasm for Your Topic

Tip 4: Sprinkle Humility Among the Expertise

Tip 5: Demonstrate Goodwill and a Desire to Give Value

Tip 6: Develop and Display a Sense of Humor

Tip 7: Don't Sermonize

Tip 8: Meet People Individually Before You Begin Your Presentation

Tip 9: Refer to People by Name During Your Presentation

Tip 10: Forget the Old Adage "Never Thank an Audience"

Tip 11: Accept Nervousness as Part of the Process

Tip 12: Use Fear to Push You to a Peak Performance

Tip 13: Use Positive Self-Talk Rather Than Focusing on the Fear

Tip 14: Find Your Fans

Tip 15: Play Mental Games of "What's the Worst?" to Overcome Disabling Fear

Tip 16: Use Physical Exercise and Activity to Release Nervous Tension

Tip 17: Concentrate on Your Audience Rather Than on Yourself to Reduce Tension

Tip 18: Don't Let Fear Mean Mediocrity

Tip 19: Be Better Than "Natural"

Tip 20: Make Your Presentation Both a Performance and a Conversation

Tip 21: Assume a Friendly Audience

Tip 22: Make Your Body Language Consistent with Your Words

Tip 23: Use Your Eyes to Build Intimacy with Audience Members One by One Randomly Around the Room

Tip 24: Think of Eye Contact as a Form of Paragraphing

Tip 25: Don't Eagle-Eye the Decision Maker

Tip 26: Use a Confident, Balanced Posture to Convey Authority

Tip 27: Use an Open Posture to Invite Participation

Tip 28: Be Aware That Gestures and Mannerisms Either Support or Sabotage What You Say

Tip 29: Study the Meanings of Common Gestures, Mannerisms, and Postures to Increase Your Awareness of Your Own Body Language

Other Resources by Dianna Booher Available from Booher Consultants

Books: Selected Titles

E-Writing: 21st Century Tools for Effective Communication

Communicate with Confidence: How to Say It Right the First Time and Every Time

Good Grief, Good Grammar

To the Letter: A Handbook of Model Letters for the Busy Executive

Great Personal Letters for Busy People

The Complete Letterwriter's Almanac

Clean Up Your Act: Effective Ways to Organize Paperwork and Get It Out of Your Life

Executive's Portfolio of Model Speeches for All Occasions

The New Secretary: How to Handle People as Well as You Handle Paper

Send Me a Memo: A Handbook of Model Memos

Writing for Technical Professionals

Winning Sales Letters

Get a Life Without Sacrificing Your Career

Ten Smart Moves for Women

Get Ahead, Stay Ahead

The Worth of a Woman's Words

Well Connected: Power Your Own Soul by Plugging into Others

Mother's Gifts to Me

The Esther Effect

Little Book of Big Questions: Answers to Life's Perplexing Questions

Love Notes: From My Heart to Yours

Fresh-Cut Flowers for a Friend

First Thing Monday Morning

Videos

Writing for Results

Writing in Sensitive Situations

Building Rapport with Your Customers

Giving and Receiving Feedback Without Punching Someone Out!

Thinking on Your Feet: What to Say During Q&A

Basic Steps for Better Business Writing (series)

Business Writing: Quick, Clear, Concise

Closing the Gap: Gender Communication Skills

Cutting Paperwork: Management Strategies

Cutting Paperwork: Support Staff Strategies

Audios

Get Your Book Published

People Power

Write to the Point: Business Communications from Memos to Meetings

Software

Selling Skills and Strategies: Write Proposals That Win the Business

Selling Skills and Strategies: Thinking on Your Feet: Handling 11 Difficult Question Types

Selling Skills and Strategies: Write to Your Buyers: Email, Letters, Reports

Selling Skills and Strategies: Create and Deliver Sales Presentations with Impact

Selling Skills and Strategies: Negotiate So That Everyone Wins

Selling Skills and Strategies: Everyone Sells: Selling Skills for the Non-Salesperson

Selling Skills and Strategies: Manage Your Pipeline, Accounts, and Time

Effective Writing

Effective Editing

Good Grief, Good Grammar

More Good Grief, Good Grammar

Ready, Set, NeGOtiate

2001 Model Business Letters

2001 Sales and Marketing Letters

8005 Model Quotes, Speeches, & Toasts

Model Personal Letters That Work

Workshops

To-The-Point E-mail and Voice Mail

Effective Writing

Technical Writing

Developing Winning Proposals

Good Grief, Good Grammar

eService Communications

Customer Service Communications

Presentations That Work (oral presentations)

People Power (interpersonal skills)

People Productivity (interpersonal skills)

Listening Until You Really Hear

Resolving Conflict without Punching Someone Out

Leading and Participating in Productive Meetings

Negotiating So That Everyone Feels Like a Winner

Increasing Your Personal Productivity

Managing Information Overload

Speeches

Communication: From Boardroom to Bedroom

From the Information Age to the Communication Age: The 10 Cs

The Gender Communication Gap: "Did You Hear What I Think I Said?"

Communicating CARE to Customers

Write This Way to Success

Platform Tips for the Presenter: Thinking on Your Feet

Get a Life Without Sacrificing Your Career

You Are Your Future: Putting Together the Puzzle of Personal Excellence

The Plan and the Purpose—Despite the Pain and the Pace

The Worth of a Woman's Words

Ten Smart Moves for Women

For More Information

Dianna Booher and her staff travel internationally presenting programs on communication and delivering motivational keynote speeches on life balance and personal productivity topics. For more information about booking Dianna or her staff, please contact:

Booher Consultants, Inc.
2051 Hughes Road.
Grapevine, TX 76051
Phone: 817-318-6000
mailroom@booher.com
www.booher.com

About the Author

Dianna Booher, CSP, is an internationally recognized business communication expert and the author of 40 books and numerous videos, audios, and an entire suite of Web-based e-learning products to improve communication, sales effectiveness, and productivity. She is the founder and president of Booher Consultants, based in the Dallas–Fort Worth Metroplex. Her firm provides keynotes and communication training (written, oral, interpersonal, gender, customer service, and sales) to some of the largest Fortune 500 companies and government agencies: IBM, ExxonMobil, Kraft, Caterpillar, PepsiCo, Frito-Lay, Nokia, JC Penney, Deloitte & Touche, Morgan Stanley, Lockheed Martin, Ernst & Young, Glaxo-SmithKline, Texas Instruments, Scientific Atlanta, MD Anderson Cancer Center, and the Army & Air Force Exchange Service, to name just a few. *Successful Meetings* magazine recently recognized her in their list of "21 Top Speakers for the 21st Century."

CPSIA information can be obtained
at www.ICGtesting.com
Printed in the USA
FSHW021800050821
83681FS